AF778183

Wills, Death and Taxes

WILLS, DEATH AND TAXES

Basic Principles for Protecting Estates

LAWRENCE W. DIXON, A.B., M.ED., M.LITT., PH.D.
Professor Emeritus of
Business Law and Wills, Trusts & Estates
Kent State University
Attorney-at-Law

REVISED EDITION

1977

LITTLEFIELD, ADAMS & CO.

Copyright © 1977
by
LITTLEFIELD, ADAMS & CO.
81 Adams Drive, Totowa, New Jersey 07512

First edition 1973
Revised edition 1977

Library of Congress Cataloging in Publication Data

Dixon, Lawrence W
Wills, death, and taxes.

(Littlefield, Adams quality paperbacks; no. 228)
Includes index.
1. Wills—United States—Popular works. 2. Decedents' estates—United States—Popular works. 3. Estate planning—United States—Popular works. I. Title.
KF755.Z9D5 1977 346'.73'056 77-21380
ISBN 0-8226-0228-8

Printed in the United States of America

Part I

LAST WILL AND TESTAMENT

Part II

PROBLEMS ENCOUNTERED AT DEATH

Part III

TAX PROBLEMS AND PROCEDURES

Preface

The old adage, "Ignorance of the law is no excuse," is neither questioned nor debated. It is the responsibility of every person who has reached the age of accountability to have an adequate knowledge of the fundamental legal principles for the purpose of protecting himself, his property, and his personal rights. Nevertheless, there is considerable evidence of failure on the part of numerous individuals possessing ownership of property to recognize the obvious disadvantages that might result from their not having a will. Such an attitude of "following the line of least resistance" while observing the "rule of thumb" approach of giving no thought of tomorrow as to the managing and caring for one's life savings could subsequently prove to represent his most serious blunder and mistake.

Only a minimum of foresight is necessary for concluding that any person who does not anticipate the possibility of certain major unforeseen difficulties (such as a sudden and unexpected death) by taking the proper precaution in drafting a will indicating to whom his property shall go following his death is guilty of gross carelessness and negligence. In the event one dies without leaving a will, the only alternative is for his entire possessions to be divided according to the law of descent and distribution; and this procedure almost invariably results in disappointments and discontent among the heirs at law.

The purpose of this book is to call to the attention of those having vested interests in property the importance of carefully providing for the eventual transfer of ownership with the least amount of inconvenience and expense. Procrastination in the drafting of one's will can often be attributed to a recognized lack of understanding of the basic legal principles involved and the possible consequences of such an oversight. In the absence of any far-sighted and serious planning, the deceased in later years, no doubt, will be remembered for his shortcomings in the care and protection of his property, as well as his failure to exercise a sympathetic attitude and sincere consideration toward the future welfare of his heirs.

A carefully-planned program of an estate requires not only the drafting of a will as a means of providing for an eventual transition of ownership of property, but it also necessitates the continuous changing, altering, and updating the "devises" and "bequests" in the will due to the inventory of the estate constantly changing because of additions, deletions, appreciation, and depreciation of certain properties. Furthermore, the moral obligations of the testator toward his beneficiaries are constantly undergoing changes due to deaths, marriages, births, and obvious needs. Such adjustments and revisions are made possible by means of drafting a new will from time to time or in the preparation of a codicil.

Part I

Last Will and Testament

Chapter 1

Exercise of Sacred Privilege

It is an obvious expectation that subsequent to one's acquiring some degree of wealth, he cannot escape giving some careful and serious consideration to the matter of choosing his successors who will eventually inherit his legal right of ownership. After experiencing certain inconveniences, sacrifices, and risks which often accompany the practice of thrift, self-denial, and consistent savings, the natural tendency of such an individual will be to exercise the highly important and satisfying privilege of preparing a document known as a will listing all beneficiaries to whom his treasured possessions will be entrusted following his death.

Recognizing the Need

The provisions in a will represent the result of serious meditation and planning by the owner of property. All who are mentioned in a will as having vested interests in the estate obviously will not be in complete accord with the wishes expressed by the testator. Instead, disappointments can be anticipated for some parties who were closely associated with the testator and entertained hopes of their being named for receiving certain bequests and devises. No person except the testator himself can account for certain personal involvements which will influence him to make definite testamentary dispositions of his property. Sometimes close relatives give the impression of their being too anxious toward gaining certain priorities which result in the testator's assuming an attitude of desiring to teach a valuable lesson to those expressing such eagerness and aggressiveness.

In view of life's uncertainties, one cannot afford to postpone planning for the future disposition of his property until there appears some form of warning signal as to his failing in health. On the contrary, he should assume more of a realistic attitude toward unforeseen possibilities by way of substituting action for procrastinating and waiting for a more opportune time. Actually, the will should be prepared when the testator seemingly is enjoying the best of health, rather than neglect such an important task until one's declining years when interested parties may unduly influence him to deviate from acting as a free and independent agent in drafting what might well be considered the most important document of his lifetime.

It is presumed that a will expresses the sincere and honest convictions of the testator. Every day of his life brings new and varied experiences with and impressions of his named beneficiaries, such as marriages, births, deaths, advancing ages, financial status of beneficiaries, and attitudes expressed toward the testator, all of which tend to constantly influence the testator to take a fresh look at his financial situation and to appraise his previous testamentary dispositions. As to the testator's estate, the inventory of his belongings is constantly changing with his acquiring, as well as the disposing, of property, the depreciation and inflation of values, and the constant variation in the residue of his estate. In order that one's will at any particular time may accurately represent his present wishes as to beneficiaries and their expressed shares of the estate, the testator should endeavor to update his will from time to time.

Purpose of a Will

A will is an instrument which conforms to the legal regulations concerning the manner in which the testator desires that his estate will be divided at his death. One who possesses property, regardless of its present value, owes a duty to prepare a will not only as a matter of personal satisfaction, but also as a convenient and time-saving medium in preparing for the eventual settling of his estate conveniently and satisfactorily. Hence, the testator at the time of executing his will is naturally concerned with the value of his estate at the particular time; and, in addition, he should anticipate his ownership of property in the future.

Making a will and indicating the parties to whom one's

property will go at the time of his death is a privilege which necessarily should be exercised with extreme caution and careful deliberation.

One might be inclined to overlook certain personal items, including household goods, clothing, jewelry, library, and automobile as to the importance often attached to the possibility of their future ownership by the testator's close of kin. In the event the beneficiary, for whom such a legacy might be intended, is not interested in acquiring the property, the court cannot enforce the transfer. In such an instance, there is little basis left for the court to determine the actual value of the legacy as to the sentimental interest which might otherwise be expressed toward the property by others who claim a vested right to its ownership.

Should the testator have relatives to whom he feels a degree of responsibility, or if there exists a charitable organization in which the testator had a particular interest, then it becomes more of a recognized personal obligation of the owner of property to designate to whom it shall go following one's death. Whenever one has marital obligations, he becomes involved in planning for the future welfare of those who are dependent on him for support and who represent the nearest of kin.

One who has ownership of property should not minimize the importance attached to his devoting a little time toward the drafting of a will indicating the manner in which his estate is to be distributed in the event of his sudden and unexpected demise. In the event of his premature decease without leaving a will, resulting in a transfer of his estate in accordance with the law of descent and distribution, the ultimate results, in all probability, would be quite unsatisfactory to the deceased had he been living at the time the distribution was made.

Opportune Time

One of the most serious mistakes for anyone, particularly a person with marital or other personal obligations, is to neglect the importance of making a will until he is convinced that the time has arrived for considering the eventual transfer of ownership of his estate. The drafting of a will, therefore, should not be the result of any contemplation of dying, but rather in anticipation of living. While a will is a device for determining how the testator's estate is to be divided at one's death, it is not the only means available for aiding and assisting the beneficiaries. Life insurance policies, with or without reservations for changing the beneficiaries at the option of the insured, should be included as an essential part and parcel of the planning process.

The owner of property may wish to designate in his will a testamentary trust by which certain beneficiaries will have only the use of the property or the income therefrom for the duration of their lives or until the happening of some designated contingency. Instead of the owner of an estate desiring to postpone until his death for certain beneficiaries to enjoy the use of some of his wealth, he may prefer to make an outright gift of some portions of his possessions or else prepare an inter vivos trust, thus enabling the beneficiaries to enjoy the use of the income from the income-producing property while the trustor is living.

The owner of property might care to concern himself as to the manner in which his estate should be shared with others in a joint tenancy, tenancy in common, tenancy in entirety, or a joint ownership and survivorship. Under a joint tenancy, tenancy in entirety, or a joint ownership and survivorship, the intention to be expressed is that the survivor would take all of such property. According to a tenancy in common form of ownership, the heirs of the deceased will inherit only the designated interests. In joint bank accounts, as well as joint ownership of government and corporate securities, the right of survivorship can be stipulated in the certificates of ownership.

Represents a Convenience—Not an Essential

Actually, there is nothing obligatory concerning one's making a will. Should he prefer, he can follow the line of least resistance and let the law take its course in having his estate divided after his death on the basis of descent and distribution. Yet, after having spent a lifetime being economical and slowly but gradually accumulating an estate, one can be expected to experience considerable satisfaction in setting forth in his will each type of property of which he is possessed and the parties to whom it is to go at his death as representing one of the highest privileges and awards which could possibly be accorded to anyone who is in possession of property irregardless of its intrinsic value. To neglect or overlook taking advantage of such a personal privilege of indicating one's successors to the ownership of his property is being very inconsiderate toward his dependents for whose future happiness and success a responsibility must be assumed.

It is safe to presume that many people procrastinate in getting down to the task of putting in writing the manner in which their property is to be divided. Oftentimes, the actual writing follows the misfortune which has befallen some close acquaintance who died without leaving a will, resulting in his estate being left in an unfortunate condition without any plan of distribution. To the other extreme, some people appear to derive considerable satisfaction from frequently bringing to the attention of beneficiaries the possibility of the testator's making changes in his will or in keeping the beneficiaries in doubt as to the actual content of his will. When certain unpleasant things have occurred or might possibly happen in the near future, the testator sometimes exercises his prerogative in threatening to draft a new will and to completely eliminate certain beneficiaries or else reduce their shares of the estate.

A testator after making a will might wish to file it away in his safety deposit box and think nothing more about the importance of his endeavoring to bring it up-to-date from time to time. Thus, he fails to consider certain important changes that should be taken into account, including the adding of new beneficiaries, removing others, acquiring additional property, deletions in his estate, and also property which has been discarded or traded. Definite changes are made possible either by the drafting of a new will or in the preparing of a codicil.

"To Err Is Human"

Failure to make a will does not constitute a violation of any legal statute or obligation. Rather, if one is negligent in designating to whom his worldly possessions will go at his death, it will have to be determined according to his marital and blood relationships. Hence, it is considered an act of carelessness and negligence in failing to provide a satisfactory plan of distribution of one's estate after death.

Should an individual desire to dispose of his property while he is living rather than bother with a will, the law might have implied under the old regulation that the gift was made in contemplation of death and apply the tax statute just as if the transfer had been testamentary. The TAX REFORM ACT of 1976 is very specific in declaring that gifts which were transacted within a period of three years of the donor's death, regardless of whether or not they were made in contemplation of death, are taxable.

Some states provide that if a transfer of property is made within two years of the transferor's death without a valuable consideration in money or money's worth for the full and adequate value of the property, such a transfer was in contemplation of death unless a contrary motive is shown. Records show that the transferor's advanced age might imply that at the time of the transfer of the property, he was aware that death was near. Consequently, the conclusion might be that the transfer was in contemplation of death.

The passing of a gentleman who was possessed with wealth in abundance created a great deal of speculation as to the approximate value of his ownership. In keeping with the accepted community custom of sitting up with the corpse, (which has not altogether disappeared in some areas), the subject of conversation centered around the good deeds of the deceased when someone raised the question as to how much wealth the deceased left behind. Quite a spontaneous answer was given by one of the members who said, "He left everything." From a legal viewpoint, it could be argued that the answer was only partially true.

Of course, the deceased cannot take his wealth with him, but at the same time he cannot leave all of it for his heirs to squabble over, since the state will likely share in its distribution. The net amount of the estate will be the gross estate less the deduction for taxes, cost of administration, funeral expenses, debts incurred from the last ailment, and debts due creditors.

Consequences of Procrastination

While one does not like to entertain negative thoughts concerning the future as to life's expectancy, yet the hard facts reveal an existing mental disturbance among all individuals as to where and under what circumstances death will strike next. This day and age with the hustle and bustle of traffic on the crowded highways, one feels very fortunate upon returning from a motor trip that he was not involved in an accident due possibly to the reckless driving of others, his own negligence in failing to observe traffic regulations, a result of his own failure to slow down while looking for directions or signs, or his failing to observe driving signals of others on an unfamiliar highway.

Many individuals are dying prematurely; and statistics reveal that on the average, wives are outliving their husbands. This conclusion can very well be attributed partly to the immense strain under which the husbands are having to work in the industrial plants, in the offices, and in the professions in an effort to make their services as productive as possible in order to insure the family's enjoyment of a higher standard of living. The existing pressure often results in young people, as well as middle-aged and elderly persons nearing the retirement age, becoming victims of heart attacks.

The general tendency of numerous young married people, who seemingly are making satisfactory progress, is that oı neglecting to give sufficient attention to certain unforeseen difficulties, such as the possibility of sudden death. One can only imagine what the future holds for the young widow, under the circumstances, with responsibilities difficult to understand unless careful planning had preceded the untimely and premature death of the head of the household. While the reality of such an occurrence is constantly within the realm of feasibility, the question cannot be overlooked or dismissed as to the qualification of a young widow who falls heir to an unpleasant environment of a similar magnitude for coping satisfactorily with the situation. Being trained to render some needed and useful service for which reasonable compensation could be assured would tend to afford a feeling of security to a young wife even though she may never have to be self-sustaining.

Parents possibly feel safer in leaving property outright to a son with the confidence of his being able to manage it successfully. As to the daughter's share of the estate, parents sometimes entertain attitudes of skepticism. They are likely to anticipate the possibility of a daughter's marriage resulting in a mismanagement of her financial affairs. As a safeguard against any such occurrences, the parents might prefer creating a testamentary trust for the daughter, thus assuring her of definite income during her lifetime.

Includes All Incidents of Ownership

Both real and personal property are included in a will. The real property represents a devise, while personal property is a bequest or legacy. The intention of the testator is usually expressed by the legal terms "give, bequeath, and devise," after which references are made to special and general legacies, followed by the disposition of the residue of the estate. Particularly when the estate is large, special devises or bequests are given; but the largest amount of the estate, usually representing the residue, will often go to a particular person who is the closest to the testator and for whom the greatest consideration is shown.

A small estate for one with very limited means is just as important to him as a much larger estate to someone who has become accustomed to thinking in terms of large-scale ownership. Consideration needs to be given not only to the successors to whom one's property will eventually go, but also when the transfers are to be made and the conditions for making them so as to protect the estate from having to pay excessive death taxes.

Naturally, there is a personal satisfaction to be derived by the testator in protecting his estate in order that his future needs will be adequately supplied. Thus, his primary consideration will involve his individual welfare; but of secondary importance is the naming of beneficiaries. If the testator has a spouse and issues, they will be expected to be the first in line to be remembered. Finally, relatives of a lower level, and possibly close friends and faithful employees over the years, may be named to share in the ultimate distribution of the estate. An individual who has succeeded in accumulating a sizeable fortune will generally develop an interest in supporting certain charities which he will be expected to remember in his will as an outright gift or in the creation of an income trust.

A conscientious family man who owns considerable wealth will be greatly concerned, as a rule, with leaving his wife the major part of his estate. Due to the possibility of the wife's having lived a very active life in rearing her children, keeping her home in order, and doing the necessary entertaining, she has been unable to acquaint herself with the problems involved in protecting an estate and in making investments. The present-day trend is more and more toward wealth getting into the possession of women who, in numerous instances, have had little or no opportunity to become familiar with general business principles which are necessary for making accurate and reliable decisions in the management of property. Such an unfortunate situation can be greatly improved through a well-organized and systematic program of future planning of one's estate.

Chapter 2

Legal Requirements of a Will

Historical records reveal that wills were known to the Greeks and Romans in the very early days of civilization. Each generation thereafter recognizing the need for a strict observance of the principles involved, has endeavored to offer improvements as to ways and means of making transfers of property after death. The guiding principles contained in the English Statute of Wills has provided a workable pattern for Probate Courts in this country, particularly in the observance of legal terminologies, formal procedures, and probation practices.

A Testator's Qualifications

The law observes the right of an individual upon reaching his majority to make a will provided he is of sound mind, disposing memory, and free of any restraint. Prior to his undertaking the task of preparing a will, it is necessary, first of all, for him to familiarize himself with the following legal requirements to be observed in the state of the testator's domicile:

(a) Except in the case of a nuncupative will, it must be in writing and signed by the testator. It can be in the testator's own handwriting if the law of that particular state recognizes holographic wills.

(b) The Probate Court prefers the type of will which is signed by the testator in the presence of two or three witnesses, according to the statutory requirements.

(c) The testator's intention must appear obvious; and while such might not be questioned, it is highly important in order to disclose his wishes in the use of the terms "give, bequeath, and devise."

(d) The will should be dated. This requirement has been recognized by courts as not representing an absolute necessity in order to establish its validity. Under some circumstances, when the testator has considered it advisable to make several wills during his lifetime, the last will, of course, will be given priority over others carrying earlier dates. Should a will not be dated, the party presenting it to the court for probation has the responsibility of proving that the writing was the testator's last will and testament.

(e) It must be signed and properly attested. The number of witnesses (two or three) required is regulated by state statute.

(f) No particular form is required; but if the traditional procedure is followed, it tends to establish reliable evidence of testamentary intention.

(g) It might be prepared in the testator's own handwriting, printed, or typewritten if the statutory provisions are complied with.

Legal Terminologies

The statute of the state in which the testator resides and calls his place of domicile has regulations which might be slightly different from procedures prescribed in other states; but the over-all principles are in keeping with a high degree of uniformity. The following general terms should be familiar to every person who has an occasion to draft or to possess a will:

(a) Testator and Testatrix. The one for whom a will is drawn is the testator, if a man; testatrix, if a woman.

(b) Devisor and Devisee. The devisor is he who transfers real property under a will; the devisee is the one for whom the transfer is intended.

(c) Legator and Legatee. The legator is he who transfers personal property under a will; the legatee is the one for whom the transfer is intended.

(d) Devise. A gift of real property by will.

(e) Legacy. Personal property mentioned in a will.

(f) Bequest. A gift of personal property by will.

(g) Executor and Executrix. The executor is a man who is mentioned in the will to execute the wishes of the testator in liquidating the estate. If the fiduciary is a woman, she is called the executrix.

(h) Administrator and Administratrix. When one makes a will but fails to mention any person to execute the will, or whenever one dies without leaving a will, in either instance the Probate Court has the responsibility of appointing someone to liquidate the estate. Such a person is the administrator if a man; or if a woman is appointed, she is called the administratrix.

(i) Testate and Intestate. One who dies leaving a will is said to have died testate; while if he dies without leaving a will, he is referred to as having died intestate.

(j) Beneficiaries. Those mentioned in the will who are to share in the estate.

(k) Codicil. A supplement to the will indicating changes, additions, or deletions.

Emphasis on Clearness

Contrary to the views of many individuals, a will does not have to conform to any particular prescribed formality in order to be effective. The most important single quality considered by the court is clearness. In other words, the court must be convinced that the document represents the intention of the testator to leave his designated earthly possessions to particular persons. If the writing has the caption: "This is My Last Will and Testament," there could be little doubt as to the testator's intention. Instead, where there is an attempt to be different and original in the drafting of one's will, the document, in the meantime, might lose its essential quality as to clearness of expression.

Such guiding principles as clearness, completeness, and exactness in the drafting of a will might be applied equally significantly to other legal documents in establishing standards of achievement. While the law does not prescribe any particular form or style for the drafting of a will, it, nevertheless, is safe to observe an accepted precedent as to formal procedure for complying with the prerequisites for insuring the necessary probation quality.

Observing Precedent

In considering the basic requirements of a will, the court is placed somewhat in the position of a mind reader in looking for evidence indicating the testator's motive. Should the court err regarding the actual purpose to be accomplished through the directives set forth in the will, the testator, meanwhile, is not around for offering any testamentary assistance. In case the will fails to measure up to the legal requirements, the estate of the deceased will pass to his heirs in accordance with the law of descent and distribution in the same manner as if no will existed.

When witnesses are called in to attest the signing of the will, the testator naturally will inform such parties that the document to which he refers represents his last will and testament. The legal procedure calls for the testator's signing first, after which it will be presented to the attesting witnesses for their signatures while in the presence of the testator and in the presence of each other. Even though the more or less customary procedure calls for the testator's signing first, after which securing the signatures of the witnesses, the courts are becoming more and more lenient in not placing too much emphasis on exactness as to the order of signing. In other words, the courts are moving away from requiring a strict observance of minor technicalities, such as expecting a specific procedure of signing a will as a prerequisite for complying with probation standards.

In a North Carolina[1] decision, a will was written on letterhead paper containing in printed words the name, place, and date. The court explained that the law of North Carolina had no statute requiring a holographic will to be dated. According to the court, the printed matter on the sheet amounted to surplusage.

A Formal Document

No uniform requirements for a will can be listed with accuracy, because circumstances would warrant the court's making exceptions from time to time to any such rules. Yet, the testator must possess the necessary mental qualities, as well as

[1] Re Lawrence's Will, 199 N.C. 782, 155 SE 876, 89 ALR (2d) 1204 (1930).

comply with the age requirements specified within the state statute. It must represent the testator's complete freedom of choosing his beneficiaries and not the result of fraud, duress, or undue influence. The provisions set forth in the will must be clear and free of any misunderstanding concerning the devisees and legatees for whom vested interests in the estate are provided.

It is obvious that the law pertaining to wills has undergone a gradual transition. In the early days, when the ability to read and write included only a comparatively few persons, oral wills were recognized. Statutes first required devises of real property to be in writing, and later the bequeaths of personal property also had to be in writing. Exceptions are generally observed as to nuncupative or oral wills made by individuals in combat duty in the armed services in revealing the content of a testator's last will and testament. Under such conditions, the various statutes regulate the making of written statements by the witnesses within a certain period of time by way of confirming the oral statement of the deceased.

In order to avoid hardship cases, state statutes in some instances recognize the validity of certain types of oral wills. On this subject, Paragraph 2107.60 of the *Ohio Revised Code* provides: "An oral will, made in the last sickness, shall be valid in respect to personal estate if reduced to writing and subscribed by two competent disinterested witnesses within ten days after the speaking of the testamentary words. Such a witness must prove that the testator was of sound mind and memory, not under restraint, and that he called upon the witnesses at the time the testamentary words were spoken to bear testimony to such disposition as his will."

Statutes Regulate Wills

One's place of domicile at the time of death will determine the interpretation of his will. Hence, the state having jurisdiction of the person will control his personal property, including that which is outside the state; but the state in which real property is located will exercise jurisdiction over it. Consequently, a will may be considered as having fulfilled all legal requirements in the state of the testator's domicile but not in the state where his real property is located. A conflict of laws results from this type of situation. A lack of uniformity of laws covering testamentary dispositions of property is somewhat overcome by the Uniform Wills Act which recognizes the laws of the state controlling the testator.

It is highly important for the testator to familiarize himself with the laws of his particular state as to the various circumstances which possibly could affect the validity of his will. For instance, if a husband at the time of his marriage had a will, in some states it could become invalid unless perhaps the premarital agreement released the wife from exercising any right of dower. In other states, the birth of a child will affect the parent's will. Actually, the testator should familiarize himself with such matters as marriage, divorce, antenuptial agreements, death of beneficiaries, births, an illegitimate child, or an adopted child.

In many instances, the common law regulations have been removed either by statute or by precedent established by courts:

(a) At common law, when a man married, his prior will was not revoked in the event no child was born. Conversely, a woman's will was revoked at the time of marriage. These wide inconsistencies have been eliminated by statutes in many states.

(b) Divorce, as a rule, will not affect the legality of one's will.

(c) Statutes regulate the influence as to the birth of a child on the validity of the testator's will.

(d) After a child has been legally adopted, statutes, as a rule, are the same as in the case of the testator's own child.

Whenever more than one page is required for the will, it is advisable that all pages be fastened together. The customary procedure, of course, is for the signing to appear on the last page. Since there is a chance for an irregularity of withdrawing pages of the will and inserting other pages as a substitute, some courts require that each page of a will contain the signature of the testator or else his initials.

Recognition of Signatures

Unless the statute so requires, the testator's signature does not have to be acknowledged under oath. Even though this practice is deemed unnecessary, there could be no opposition by the court toward such procedure. The general accepted custom has been for the testator and the witnesses to perform the signing in the presence of each other.

The manner of acknowledging signatures in a will is of importance to the court. However, the courts are constantly faced with varied deviations from the general rule of signing. Under some conditions, someone may sign for the testator provided it was done at his request, as well as in his presence. Other courts maintain that even though the signing for the testator was not done in his presence, but later was acknowledged by him, was accepted as being legal.

Legality of Mark or Symbol for Signatures

State laws vary as to the legality of signatures by a mark or symbol. A court naturally would entertain great suspicion should the testator, instead of writing his signature, indicate the signing with a mark or symbol. Whenever a testator is unable to write his name, due to physical or educational reasons, the safest procedure for him would be to offer a mark or symbol to represent his signature while in the presence of two or more witnesses who subscribed their names thereto in the presence of a notary public who, in turn, certified the mark or symbol as representing the signature of the testator.

Questions as to the legality of a will are also expected to be raised when the testator's name is typewritten. This, too, would necessitate the witnessing of the signature for the sake of clearness of intention. Actually, courts are known to be in disagreement as to what amounts to clear and convincing evidence relative to the proper and acceptable procedure for witnessing a signature.

When the testator authorizes his signature in his will to be signed by someone else, the courts will always consider the possibility of existing irregularities as constituting acts of fraud and bad faith. A Kentucky[2] court was faced with the problem of the signing by the testator and the witnesses in the presence of each other; but the witnesses signed first, after which the testator signed his name. The court explained that a point could not be made of the fact that the witnesses signed before the testator, because, according to the court, the order of signing was insignificant and not affecting the legality of the will.

A requirement of a will is that it must be signed by the testator, but the statutes fail to prescribe any particular place

---

[2] Hapson v. Ewing, 353 SW 203, 91 ALR (2d) 733 (1961).

on the will for signing. Hence, it might be implied that the signature could appear any place on the will, assuming that it could be proven that the signature was genuine. In the interest of clearness, however, it is preferred that the testator follow the customary procedure of having the signature of the testator, as well as the names of attesting witnesses, appear at the end of the will.

Selecting Witnesses

Statutes differ in the various states relative to the number of attesting witnesses necessary in a will. Some states require two while other states require three. As a matter of precaution, unless one is certain as to the exact requirement, it is preferred to have more witnesses than are required by law than to have too few. Allowances may be made for deaths, incapacitation, unable to appear in court at probation time, disqualification, or perhaps the possibility of the moving of the witness from the particular area. On occasions, the court may not require that all of the witnesses appear to testify as to the genuineness of the testator's signature.

Qualification of a Witness

To qualify as a competent attesting witness, one must not be an interested party in the estate of the testator. This disqualification might be offset by having enough additional competent witnesses for fulfilling the legal requirements as to the number required. There is always a possibility of one or more witnesses being declared by the court as incompetent to acknowledge the signature of the testator. One who is mentioned in the will of the testator as a legatee, a devisee, or in some manner hopes to realize some financial advantage from the estate will be disqualified from serving in this capacity.

Husband and wife have been declared incompetent to testify for or against each other because of their personal interests which would tend to influence them to be biased and unreliable. This recognized incompetency, no doubt, would be discovered in the attitude of husband or wife toward the will of the other. The theory of disqualifying one as a witness on the basis of personal interest would naturally include husband and wife.

Generally speaking, the fact that a person is mentioned as an executor or executrix in a will does not disqualify him or her as an attesting witness provided his or her rate of compensation is a stipulated amount. Since competency of a witness is determined at the time of the attestation, it is reasoned that in mentioning an executor or executrix in a will of the testator merely amounts to a recommendation which will need the confirmation of the court before it becomes legal. Thus, the executor qualifies as a witness before his acceptance as an executor.

An attorney at law is qualified to attest the will which he has prepared provided the testator makes such request. The particular service rendered does not disqualify him from testifying at the time the will is probated. Courts have gone so far as not to disqualify an attorney from attesting the signature because of his employment as legal adviser to the executor. The confirmation of the executor would follow the signing as an attesting witness, and the appointment would have to get the approval of the court.

A Complete Instrument

Courts are divided when additional witnesses later sign. Many courts are long on upholding a strict enforcement of the law even if it results in invoking hardships. Exceptions have been made if the attesting witnesses were in the room or adjoining rooms at the time of the testator's signing. In an Arizona[3] controversy, one of the witnesses signed the will of the testator and then left the house without witnessing the signing by the testator. Also, the witness had never been informed as to the testator's signing. The court did not consider this act as a compliance with the statutory law of the state which required the testator's signature, or by some other person designated to sign for the testator in his presence and at his request.

Also, the Arizona statute provided that the will must be attested by two or more credible witnesses over fourteen years of age. The court called attention to one line of authority which held that the will was not valid unless the testator signed first and then the attesting witnesses signed in the presence of each other. Another authority considered the order of signing

---

[3] Re Brashear's Estate, 54 Ariz. 430, 96 P (2d) 747 (1939).

as being immaterial. In the present case, the court held that the will was invalid because a witness was not present to acknowledge the testator's signature.

The will is considered as having been published when its content is made known. Presenting it to attesting witnesses stating that it represented the testator's last will and testament is sufficient. Should the will be read in the presence of the testator and the attesting witnesses and the testator expressed his approval by word or deed, it amounts to a publication. Also, a gesture made by the testator as to where the signature of the witness should go has been held sufficient for constituting a publication.

Promise to Name Beneficiaries

When all of the requirements of a contract for making a will have been complied with, failure to execute the will in accordance with the terms agreed to, which were conditions precedent, affords the injured party with certain privileges for receiving recourse: (1) Go into a court of law and bring an action for damages for breach of contract; (2) Petition the court of equity for specific performance; (3) If the transfer has been made to someone else who is in possession, a request could be made to the court to declare the one in possession as the trustee for the benefit of the claimant as the beneficiary.

A meeting of the minds constitutes a mutual agreement, and all of the essentials must be present before there can be a binding and enforceable contract. In the event one of the parties breaches his promise, he becomes liable to the other in the form of monetary damages; and if this should be considered inadequate compensation as a remedy, he may take the matter to a court of equity and secure an order of specific performance.

A will, on the other hand, constitutes a voluntary act and can be revoked, altered, or changed at any time while the testator is living. Even though the purpose of a contract and a will ordinarily are separate and distinct, nevertheless, the law does not prohibit their being used as a combination for attaining an objective. Although an occasion seldom arises which necessitates such practice, the procedure is feasible and practicable. There is nothing which is prohibitory to the testator's mentioning in his will that a certain described legacy is based on specific consideration and constitutes a binding contract.

If one makes a gratuitous promise to remember someone

in his will, this is not enforceable since it is not supported by consideration. Yet, if a property owner agrees to make a will leaving a party certain designated property in consideration of a detriment to be suffered by the promisee, such as surrendering the title to certain property or a commitment to take care of the promisor during his lifetime, the promise is legal and binding. Should the testator promise to leave his farm to his son in return for which the son promises to care for his father during the rest of his life, the contract is enforceable. It would be difficult to prove the existence of such a contract in the absence of any writing to that effect. Some statutes prescribe (and wisely so) that an agreement to make a devise or bequest in one's will of certain property has no legal effect unless it is in writing.

While the law recognizes the right of a person to contract to devise real property or to bequeath personal property in his will to designated individuals, the contract might also apply to one's not leaving property in his will, resulting in the subsequent dividing of his estate under the law of descent and distribution. In such wise, a contract would be recognized by the courts, assuming that the motive is valid and not based on acts of fraud, deceit, duress, or undue influence.

Chapter 3

Essential Qualities of a Will

The law regarding the legal right of a property owner to make a will is considered very reasonable. The general rule is that every individual is accorded such a right provided he is empowered with the necessary mental capacity. While the moral standard of some people might be quite low, it, nevertheless, would be a rather difficult task for the court to determine the degree of morality essential to qualify one for exercising this privilege. Much consideration is given by the courts in establishing the capacity of a reasonable person under similar circumstances.

Expression of Testator's Wishes

Much has been written in an effort to accurately describe the necessary mental capacity of a testator for making a will, but no reliable standard for measurement has been established. Actually, one may qualify under some conceived standard but prove quite deficient under others. The basis for judging the competency of a testator might be determined by his understanding of the purpose of his making the disposition according to his own personal wishes and convictions.

In judging the mental capacity of an individual to make a will, it cannot be expected that he understands all legal requirements involved for assuring probation quality. The purpose of anyone's soliciting the assistance of legal counsel is to make more certain of his conforming to all legal standards. The mere fact that the testator has expressed an interest in drafting a will is evidence of his possessing a sense of accomplishment in identifying the devisees and legatees of his estate.

The basic legal principles governing the testator's competency for drafting a will concern his having reached his majority and being possessed with a sound mind and disposing memory. Ordinarily, infants are not granted that privilege; although the common law recognized males fourteen years of age and females twelve years of age as being entitled to this right. The common law prohibited one convicted of a felony from making a will, but that restriction has more or less been removed. A married woman, as a rule, has the right to dispose of her property by will. This represents a deviation from the common law which gave her the right to dispose of her personal property provided the husband gave his consent. Aliens are generally granted the right to leave their property to others by means of a will.

It is more or less expected that for one to qualify for having the necessary capacity for making a will, he should possess full and complete knowledge as to the extent of his ownership and also his motives for mentioning certain beneficiaries. This would not necessarily imply that the testator must show a familiarity with all of the facts and details concerning his right of ownership.

Partial Incompetency for Making a Will

One's testamentary capacity for drafting a will can be judged by his ability and capacity for practicing a profession, operating a business, or negotiating contracts. Insofar as his illiteracy test is concerned, his rating may be rather low; nevertheless, he could qualify under certain standards for making a testamentary disposition of his estate to become effective at his death. Neither should physical handicaps disqualify one for making a will. Also, the person who is blind, deaf, and dumb has an equal right to decide to whom his property will eventually descend.

One's privilege to make a will cannot be destroyed on the ground of his limited educational advantages. Despite the fact that he is unable to read and write and his speech is very crude and unintelligible, the court will be inclined to rely on the obvious convictions of the testator toward providing for the testamentary disposition of his property. In such an instance, the responsibility of the court would be that of determining if some person was guilty of misrepresentation, fraud, duress, or unduly influencing the illiterate.

The fact that a person is blind or deaf should not necessarily disqualify him from making a testamentary disposition of his property. People suffering from such handicaps are being rehabilitated with present-day methods so that they are capable of making worthwhile contributions to society. On occasions, they are in a favorable position for accumulating wealth, as well as adding to that which has been left to them. Under such circumstances, certainly they should not be deprived of the opportunity of drafting a will.

A convict has been recognized as having the right to dispose of his property. Even though the sentence is for life, he should have the privilege of making a will which will be enforceable at his death.

Frequently, the testator in his introductory statement will refer to his being of sound mind and disposing memory; but this is more of a customary common law formality. In this respect, attention might be focused on an individual who was intoxicated at the time the will was prepared or who had arrived at an advanced age resulting in his mental faculties becoming somewhat retarded. The Probate Court, meanwhile, will likely declare the testator to be competent; but this presumption might be rebutted by evidence showing the contrary to be true. The law throws the strong arm of protection around those who are partially incompetent for entering into certain transactions by way of protecting them from those who would delight in exercising undue influence in an effort to exploit them.

Judging Capacity of a Witness

Courts have held that a minor is capable of signing a will in the capacity of an attesting witness. In a Nebraska[1] case, it was decided that a minor fourteen years of age was qualified to sign as a witness. Other courts have ruled that a child under fourteen years of age was incompetent to act as a subscribing witness; but that presumption, according to some courts, is subject to being rebutted.

[1] Spier v. Spier, 99 Neb. 853, 157 NW 1014 (1930).

Even if a witness is a member of some fraternal, social, or religious organization which is included in the will as a beneficiary, his competency, as a rule, will not be affected. But where a will goes so far as to mention an attesting witness as a trustee with unlimited authority to manage the trust according to his desire, this additional responsibility will tend to disqualify such a party from serving as an attesting witness.

It is generally held that an executor who has no interest in the estate of the testator, other than his income from liquidating the estate, is competent to witness the testator's signing his will. This would be equivalent to the testator's signing as an unbiased individual, since he would be interested primarily in executing the provisions set forth in the testator's will.

Whenever one has a vested interest as a devisee or a legatee in a will in which he is an attesting witness, this presents a real problem which the statute of the state or the court must decide. The logic which has been applied by the courts to a situation of this type has been that a beneficiary could not witness the portion of the estate intended for himself personally; consequently, he would be disqualified as an attesting witness.

Functions of Executor

The executor is mentioned in the will to execute the wishes and directives of the testator. The rendering of this service is on a purely voluntary basis. In order that the testator may have reasonable assurance that the executor will assume this responsibility, it is logical to assume that first of all an inquiry should be made of the executor concerning his willingness to serve in this capacity.

Complete authority of the executor cannot be anticipated in detail. Mentioning in the testator's will merely the name of the executor amounts to a nomination which will have to be confirmed by the court. Objections to the confirmation may be offered by the beneficiaries who either distrust the executor or else they consider him to be incompetent to serve efficiently in this capacity.

Should a wife possess the necessary knowledge and experience for looking after the husband's estate, she may be entrusted with the responsibility of being named the executrix. Oftentimes the husband does not consider his wife to be capable of executing the provisions of his will, or he possibly might reason that she did not have the necessary time to devote to this extra function because of her duties in caring for her children. In case the entire estate of the husband is to go to his widow, it is to be expected that she will be named the executrix unless, perhaps, the estate is rather involved or the wife is quite deficient in understanding basic business principles.

Subject to Revocation

Prior to the testator's incorporating his plan into a formal written document for dividing his estate, he naturally will devote considerable time concerning how such decisions should be made. His individual act is an implication that he is following the dictates of his own conscience and that the decisions represent his own free will and accord. Consequently, the presumption is that he is not driven by any compulsion, force, fraud, duress, or undue influence. During one's lifetime, he may conclude that because of certain changes having been made in his estate, his will needs to be revamped from time to time. The court will always give priority to the will possessing the most recent date.

Chapter 4

Types of Wills

Contrary to the belief of the average layman that a will should be quite detailed and sprinkled with a number of high-sounding and hackneyed terms commonly found in legal documents, it must be remembered that the court's chief concern is in gaining a clear conception of the testator's actual wishes.

An example of a very brief will which was brought before the Probate Court of a southern state for probation contained the following: "What is mine is my wife's." In passing favorably on the will for probation, the court concluded that the writing expressed the intention of the testator. Even though the will passed all requirements of this particular court, such brevity should not be recommended or encouraged. It might lead to misunderstanding of interpretation in determining, first of all, if the writing was intended as a will or whether it was merely a passing remark and lacking in genuine serious intention. One might also inquire if the provision in the will applied only to the property the testator possessed at the time of executing the will or was it intended to include all after-acquired property as well.

Holographic Will

A will which is prepared in one's own handwriting should conform to all statutory requirements, as it will have to be approved for probation with the same formality as any other form of testamentary disposition. Following the death of a President of the United States, a question was raised in the press regarding whether or not he left a will. The inference was made that the immediate members of his family were not kept informed as to his testamentary decisions. Shortly thereafter it was reported that a will written in the testator's own handwriting on White House stationery was found by the law partner of the deceased. The carefully-chosen words comprising only a single sentence were as follows: "Not unmindful of my son, ______, I give, bequeath, and devise all of my property, real, personal, and mixed, to my wife, ______, to hold in fee simple." A question was raised in the press at the time concerning the meaning of the expression, "Not unmindful of my son, ______,." A few days thereafter this matter was clarified in a follow-up statement explaining that a trust fund had been created for the son's portion of the estate.

Some states do not require a holographic will, which is executed by the testator in his own handwriting, to be witnessed. However, other states insist that such a will be witnessed just the same as wills not drafted in the testator's handwriting.

In an effort to comply with the Utah[1] statutory requirement of a holographic will, the blank spaces in a standard testamentary form were filled in by the testatrix's own handwriting. The court contended that the statutory law pertaining to a holographic will had been complied with even though the standard printed form contained certain printed matter. The assumption was made to the court that in order to constitute a holographic will, only the written words and figures could be offered for probation. On the contrary, the court held that the printed material was a vital part of the will just as much as the script which had been filled in by the testatrix.

Courts have also contended that while the requirements of a holographic will provide that the instrument must be written wholly by the testator, yet if some of the data are printed, the validity of the instrument is not questioned. For example, where it is written on stationery with a printed heading containing the name of the city, state, and provisions for the particular month and year, such as 19______, with the figure for the year to be filled in, the validity of the will would not be affected, as a general rule, since the statutes usually do not require that the will be dated for probation.

While a holographic will in a particular state might be probated without the signatures of attesting witnesses, it would

---

[1] Re Wolcott, 54 Utah 165, 180 P 169, 80 ALR 1205 (1919).

represent the exercise of extra precaution in having it properly witnessed. Since questions are sometimes raised as to the drafting of a holographic will on a printed form, it is to be preferred, of course, that the entire content of a holographic will be in the testator's own handwriting in order to avoid any grounds for contesting the probation of the will on the grounds of irregularity as to form.

In looking for a justifiable cause for objecting to the probation of a will, questions might also be raised as to the use of a rubber stamp. This possibility of criticism as to the form and content of the will might invariably appear quite obvious, and the testator should necessarily take precautionary measures for guarding against such negligence and carelessness.

Nuncupative Will

As a rule, a will must be in writing and in compliance with the statutory requirements in order to be effective for probation. Exceptions are made under certain conditions for members of the armed forces. When such a person is engaged in combat duty, and realizing the full danger which he is undergoing and the possibility of his meeting with death at any moment, he may possess a strong urge to make known to his associates, as witnesses, that should he not survive, he desired to have his earthly belongings go to designated parties or organizations.

In the event the testator dies, and the witnesses appear to confirm the oral declaration of disposition by a writing according to the statutory requirements, the court will consider the quality of the will for probation. Particularly, when there are no objections offered by interested parties, the court will entertain little hesitancy in giving the will probation recognition.

It is usually provided in most jurisdictions that the nuncupative will must be reduced to writing within a certain number of days after it was made so that the witnesses will not forget or confuse the content of the will. Courts are quite reluctant to recognize an oral will which was made under such unusual and trying circumstances, as there is little opportunity for verifying the accuracy of such a disposition. Furthermore, even if the witnesses were sincere, the conditions which prompted the expression of an intention to make a testamentary disposition of property would likely influence the court to allow for inaccuracies and confusion on the part of the witnesses in recalling all of the facts.

Joint Will

Particularly when two or more individuals own property jointly, they may be concerned in making a joint will in which they will recognize the right of the survivor to acquire the ownership in its entirety. Similarly, two or more persons who possess different and separate holdings agree as to the right of survivorship. Also, two persons may draft separate wills, and each one will mention the other as beneficiary. Conditions would have to be very unusual to justify individuals in drafting wills jointly with others with the right of survivorship except in the case of husband and wife who desire to indicate their joint ownership in property with the right of survivorship. When two or more persons possessing a common ownership, other than husband and wife, desire to make such a will with survivorship rights, it is sometimes stipulated in the will that it cannot be revoked or altered except with the consent of all of the other parties.

Mystic Will

Such a will is often drafted on a printed form and signed by the testator in the presence of the attesting witnesses who, in turn, attest the signing in the presence of the testator and of each other. This is a formal expression by the testator and is preferred over the informal holographic will. Caution must be exercised in complying with the statutory requirements, particularly as to the number of witnesses, as well as the qualifications of the parties involved in the will, such as the witnesses, the testator, the executor, and possibly the trustee in case a testamentary trust is included in the will.

Conditional Will

A prerequisite is stipulated in such a will in the form of a condition or a contingency which will have to be complied with before the will becomes effective. As a rule, one should entertain considerable skepticism in becoming involved in a testamentary disposition of this description. There always exists an element of uncertainty as to its meriting probation quality.

A Codicil

A codicil represents an addition to or a deletion from the will, and is either attached to the will or describes it in such a manner as to indicate an intention that the writing is a supplement to the original document.

Chapter 5

Guide in Drafting a Will

There exists a possibility of a testator's failure to provide the necessary safeguards against certain inconveniences which might be suffered by beneficiaries following one's death. When the estate, by necessity, comes under the guardianship and control of the Probate Court for a comparatively long period of time, the delayed action is certain to result in disappointments and the loss of privation for those having vested interests. This type of burden, which often results from a premature and sudden death, can be partially overcome quite simply by way of exercising foresight in the drafting of a will.

Securing Advice and Counsel

A will may be unusually brief but at the same time very clear and definite in expressing the testator's wishes. Again, it could be quite long, detailed, and incoherent, resulting in confusion, delay, and difficulty of interpreting by the court. Unless the estate is rather large and includes a wide variety of property ownership and the naming of a number of beneficiaries, the task of drafting a will should require little effort. However, conditions frequently inserted by the testator who has limited knowledge of the legal principles involved can cause the document to appear quite wordy and complicated. The safest procedure, of course, is to rely on the counsel and guidance of an attorney. Meanwhile, the results will be more satisfying to the testator when he possesses a practical understanding of the law of wills which will enable him to foresee the need for an intelligent and knowledgeable planning of his estate.

When the ownership is quite involved, perhaps the testator will not wish to entrust the counsel to any one type of professional person. In addition to his securing the advice of an attorney, perhaps an accountant could contribute a great deal of constructive advice insofar as ways and means for savings in the form of taxes. Particularly, if a testator is concerned with the creation of a trusteeship, a banker or an officer in an investment trust concern may be able to make a worthwhile contribution.

The responsibility of a testator, while in the stage of contemplating the drafting of a will, should make certain of his observing a well-organized plan of procedure, such as:

(a) Prepare an inventory of all real and personal property owned by the testator.
(b) List all legatees of the personal property and the devisees of the real property.
(c) Provision for the payment of the state inheritance tax and possibly the federal estate tax (provided the taxable estate is sufficiently large) from a specific fund.
(d) Indicate if the estate is to be left outright to beneficiaries or whether a trusteeship is to be created.
(e) Arrange for a portion of the estate to be included in the residue.

Description of Property

Included in the testator's will can be any right of ownership possessing intrinsic value. Generally speaking, the owner of property has the satisfaction of disposing of his estate in any manner which seemingly will bring him the greatest amount of personal satisfaction. There exists, moreover, a definite right of his spouse which cannot be ignored. Hence, he cannot dispose of his real estate without getting her acquiescence; otherwise, she will be privileged to maintain her dower interest at the husband's death. If the state of her domicile recognizes community property, she can claim ownership to the extent of one-half of the estate acquired during their marriage.

The testator cannot leave outright in his will property which he does not own even though he is reasonably certain of acquiring it eventually. For example, a parent drafts a will leaving everything to his only child. Yet, there is no absolute assurance that the parent will not change his or her mind in canceling the will or in revoking it by drafting a new will or a codicil. Many possibilities could be enumerated that might influence the parent in drafting a new will, thereby reducing the amount which the child is to receive. What one expects to eventually acquire, he may create a testamentary trust for the benefit of his wife and allow her full authority to dispose of the estate in any manner she may consider advisable and reasonable.

A testator must always keep in mind that his estate is constantly undergoing a change due to his acquiring new property, as well as the continuous process of disposing of property from time to time by means of selling, discarding, or destroying it. Allowances will also have to be made for changes in the value of certain property due to depreciation, obsolescence, or fluctuations in the prices of such products on the open market. Naturally, a will is not going to be changed every time the value of ownership to property fluctuates one way or the other.

Priorities of Distribution

The law assumes that the debts of the deceased will be settled before the legatees, devisees, or heirs will be entitled to their shares of the estate. The will, in fact, may indicate that the debts, funeral expenses, and cost of administration will be settled before the beneficiaries are entitled to their interests. The testator has the privilege of designating the part of the estate out of which such deductions from the gross estate will be paid.

Whenever the husband makes a will, he often fails to consider the possibility of his surviving his spouse. Assuming that the wife owns considerable property, the husband will be entitled only to the statutory amount of her estate, should he survive her, with the remainder going to her bodily heirs; and in the absence of any such heirs, to the next of kin of the deceased. A protection against anything like this occurring is for the wife, as well as the husband, to make a will whereby the beneficiaries, to whom certain property will go at the time of death, will be clearly expressed.

Despite the fact that all individuals possessing property are urged to make testamentary dispositions of such ownership, there are sometimes occasions for their not desiring to do so. A wife, for example, sometimes entertains a selfish attitude toward expecting her spouse to leave her everything. If the husband believes otherwise and procrastinates in preparing a will, all the wife will be able to receive at her husband's death will be her legal inheritance under the law of descent and distribution. The owner of property may reason that an observance of the statutory regulations would come nearer satisfying his personal wishes than in assuming a discriminating attitude in naming beneficiaries.

A big responsibility rests on the testator in drafting his will. He must necessarily take into consideration the needs of those whose future welfare will depend to a great degree on the nature of the decisions made in the drafting of his will. He might conclude that present circumstances would tend to indicate a number of useful and productive years for the testator; but, meanwhile, he must consider also the present needs of his beneficiaries should he die prematurely. Standards for determining rights of beneficiaries might be on the basis of age, sex, capacity to care for the property, experience in making business decisions, type of property involved, and the value of the estate.

Observing Formalities

Individuals have become accustomed to observing legal formalities and terminologies as being essential in the drafting of wills. Actually, they entertain considerable skepticism toward planning for the future because of the legal technicalities involved. Such a narrow-sighted attitude of failing to anticipate unpleasant happenings in the future is gradually being substituted by more of a thoughtful and realistic outlook toward the future. It is not essential, for example, to state, "This is my last will and testament," as this is to be implied from the date of the document. Actually, the introductory remark is a descriptive expression and connotes an element of completeness and exactness when it is included.

The simplest thing for a testator to do in drafting his will is to leave his property outright to designated beneficiaries, but circumstances may alter this procedure in view of certain beneficiaries possessing incapacities in caring for property intended for them. Under such conditions, it might be deemed necessary to create a trusteeship for making an assignment of property to trustees for the benefit of certain beneficiaries and to provide for the payment of income to particular parties for a definite period of time or until the happening of designated contingencies. Still another possibility might be to appoint a testamentary guardian to look after the beneficiary and his property until the deficiency is corrected.

In drafting a will, one must always bear in mind that the Probate Court will have the responsibility of making the decision as to the quality and content of the document relative to its qualifying for probation. First of all, emphasis should be given to the conveying of the correct meaning. The court cannot always visualize just what the testator had in mind by expressions which are not definite and concise. Conditions in one's will should be kept to a minimum. While the sincerity of the testator can be appreciated, he may, at the same time, fail to make prominent in the mind of the court, as well as parties with vested interests, that which is uppermost in his own mind.

Content of a Will

While there is no uniformity prescribed by statute or any decisional law for the drafting of a will, it is always preferred that some standard of procedure be observed. The basic essentials of a will can be more meaningful and better understood by carefully observing the general principles involved:

(a) *The Heading or Caption.* By way of emphasizing clearness of expression as to the purpose of preparing the instrument, descriptive terms are often used:

"Last Will and Testament"
"This Is My Last Will and Testament"
"Last Will and Testament of ———"

(b) *Introductory Clause.* The testator discloses his intention of making the instrument his last will and testament.

(c) *Naming Devisees and Legatees.* In a will, the gift of real property is known as a devise, and the beneficiary is a devisee; while a gift of personal property is a bequest, the property is a legacy, and the beneficiary is a legatee.

(d) *Testimonium Clause.* It is referred to as the attesting clause by which the testator acknowledges, by his signature, his approval as to the content of the will.

(e) *Testatum Clause.* The witnesses signify that the testator signed, published, and declared the document to be his last will and testament; and at his request, they subscribed their names as attesting witnesses.

A Safeguard for One's Will

As a protection, the testator may deposit his will with the Probate Court of the county in which one's domicile is established. Considering the availability of photostatic machines for duplication purposes, a testator should exercise precaution in having for himself a copy, as a matter of evidence and also of content, for subsequent updating of his will when considered necessary. The inconvenience to the testator when a new will, or a codicil, is prepared in not having available a copy of the old will as a guide is an argument in favor of his keeping a copy of such an important instrument with his other valuable papers. A testator would be acting very unwisely and without proper foresight in having a will without making known to his beneficiaries as to where it is kept for safety reasons, particularly when it is not filed in the customary place where other important documents are kept.

Particularly, whenever a lawyer is employed to draw up the will in which he might be mentioned as an executor, and possibly a trustee, a copy of the will could conveniently be left in his care. This would make it very advantageous for the attorney to file the will for probation at the death of the testator. In the event the attorney predeceases the testator, or else becomes incapacitated and unable to serve efficiently, there should be no delay on the part of the testator in acting with vigilance in drafting a new will.

Chapter 6

Expression of Testator's Intention

As in preparing any other legal document, it is preferred and recommended that some precedent as to formality of procedure be observed in the drafting of one's will, although this is not considered an absolute necessity. The court's concern, to be sure, is to discover the testator's mental reaction at the time the will was executed; and the only means available is to observe the language used in conveying his ideas. There could be no possible confusion relative to what the testator meant by an introductory statement, "This is my last will and testament." Naturally, the expression prepares the reader for the factual data to follow.

Allowances for Future Estate Changes

Controversies arise concerning the disposition of property acquired by the testator subsequent to the execution of his will. If the estate has been greatly affected over the years by such factors as depreciation, obsolescence, subject to a trade-in or a sale, or the fluctuation of the market value, the testator may wish to avoid possible confusion and ill-feeling among beneficiaries by way of preparing a new will from time to time or in drafting a codicil. It is to be remembered that the effectiveness of a will dates from the time of probation and not the period of its execution.

Actually, the testator has complete authority to set forth any suppositions in his testamentary gifts of property. The type of conditions, of course, will be in accordance with his wishes and interests. It would very well apply to the legatees' reaching particular ages, the date of marriages, or upon the happening of some certain event. The speculations might fall within the categories of "conditions precedent" or "conditions subsequent." In the former, a certain act will have to be complied with before the title and possession pass to the property in question. In the latter, the possession passes to the legatees with the understanding that absolute ownership will not pass until the condition is subsequently complied with.

It is the responsibility of the court to make presumptions as to what the testator intended by the use of various expressions in his will. If portions of the estate are not mentioned in the testator's will, possibly due to his having acquired certain property following the execution of his will, the court could not endeavor to observe the intention as set forth in the will before drawing any conclusion as to whom the property should go. Under no circumstances could the court contend that property not mentioned in the will must escheat to the state.

Exercising Right of Ownership

Considerable satisfaction naturally comes to one who has acquired absolute ownership of property in that he can do with it as he pleases so long as hardships are not inflicted on others. It is reasonable to assume that a property owner will desire to name his successors to the future ownership of his estate. Close of kin, of course, are expected to be accorded favorable consideration when the will is probated; but the testator may choose not to disclose to his beneficiaries the content of his will for fear of creating within them suspicion, jealousy, and discontent. The attitude assumed by the testator toward close blood relatives will be disclosed in allowing them considerable priority in the distribution of his estate, but the obligation is merely moral and not legal.

A property owner derives pleasure and contentment in being able to maintain that his right of ownership entitles him to the privilege of determining his personal plan of disposition of his estate. It is possible that he will select one or more of several alternatives for eventually bringing about the transition, such as: a testamentary gift; a testamentary dedication for some charitable, religious, educational, or scientific purpose; an outright gift; a testamentary or inter vivos trust. When an outright gift is made, the owner loses his right of dominion over the property, while in a revocable inter vivos trust, a reservation can be made to change, alter, or revoke the trust at the trustor's discretion. Furthermore, one may wish to establish a joint tenancy or tenancy by entirety by which the survivor takes all.

The general significance of a will follows a similar pattern. Yet, it is seldom that a particular form for wills could be conveniently used in its entirety for all situations unless the testator observed the principle of complete simplicity in leaving all of his estate to a particular person, such as his spouse. The purpose to be accomplished is to protect the interests of those whose welfare depends largely on the planning and forethought of the testator. In executing this task, the testator comes face to face with the needs of beneficiaries, particularly those who are the closest to him.

The description of real property in a will does not require the degree of accuracy as would be expected in a deed of conveyance. Actually, the testator might leave all of his real property to a particular person, and this would include such ownership of which he is seized at the time of death. In similar instances, a deed could not be so general. In a large acreage of land contained in one's will, for example, which is left in equal shares to more than one person, the court would be able to ascertain the testator's intention; but in a deed of conveyance, the grantor could not be so vague and indefinite.

Observing Statutory Provisions

The privilege accorded the testator to change, alter, revoke, mutilate, or destroy his will exists until death. The law of his particular state of domicile prescribes definite requirements of a will which must be satisfied before probation is allowed. Courts are always concerned with the intention of the testator, as well as an observance of all regulations. Particularly, when the testator is uncertain regarding the legal aspects of his will, a competent attorney, perhaps, should be engaged to draft the will according to the testator's interests and in keeping with all statutory regulations.

No definite rules are prescribed for the drafting of a will. Rather, the courts do not emphasize technical legal terminologies in the construction of wills. The court is left no other alternative than to conclude that the testator knew his own mind in indicating how his estate is to be divided and for whom specific property is intended. Should the court experience difficulty in determining the actual meaning intended by the testator resulting from the use of certain ambiguities and inconsistencies, the only authority to which to refer will be the statutory regulations under the principle of descent and distribution. There is always a chance that something might hinder the probation of the will. Even though a simpler and safer method for disposing of one's property, perhaps, would be in making an outright inter vivos gift; but the disadvantages to the donor would be his loss of security from further exercising ownership over the property, as well as his losing control over it thereafter.

Provisions of the Will

Beneficiaries in a will are sometimes described merely as "my beloved husband," "my dear wife," "my son," "my daughter," "my children," etc. For the sake of clearness, both the name and degree of the relationship should be mentioned. Merely referring to the state of kinship will be perfectly clear at the time of the execution of the will; but after the lapse of a number of years prior to the time of probation, the relation expressions will perhaps take on different connotations of meaning due to changes having taken place, such as deaths, births, divorces, and remarriages.

Under the common law, property devised or bequeathed in the testator's will was revoked when the testator surrendered his right of ownership to the property. The principle was based on the assumption that whenever the property was mentioned in the testator's will at the time of execution, the expectation was that such designation of transfer was to continue until death. In case the right of the beneficiary was altered by way of disposing of the property, the devise or bequeath, as set forth in the will, became revoked. Should the property be later reacquired, the question was whether or not the original devise or bequeath became effective. Many statutes regulate the after-acquired property by way of including the extent of ownership at the time of the testator's death.

Even though it is not obligatory that the will must conform to a definite pattern of expressions, it is always preferred that the instrument denote adequate clearness of purpose in order to avoid any possible misconception relative to proper interpretation. The courts, therefore, are more concerned with the impressions conveyed from the words and expressions used in the will rather than emphasizing strict grammatical construction of words and terms employed. Most important for the court is that of discovering the objectives of the testator. Even though the grammar used in the will might indicate a high degree of illiteracy on the part of the testator, yet, the court's problem is to analyze the expressions used for discovering the testator's wishes.

Special Designations

Assuming that a will may clearly describe the manner in which the estate is to be bequeathed and devised, certain designations will be specific while others will be general. A specific legacy or devise may describe particular property, such as a farm, household goods, securities, etc., which are intended for particular beneficiaries. A general legacy or devise makes reference as to the proportionate amount of certain property which beneficiaries will receive, such as leaving a farm or securities in trust for the testator's minor children.

The primary concern of a testator is to designate particular individuals or organizations as beneficiaries of specific property to become effective at the testator's death unless the will is altered or revoked.

Reference to Residue

The will includes the special and general legacies, as well as the residue of the estate. Yet, some wills omit the residue, resulting in that portion of the estate, not covered in the testator's will, to be divided by the law of descent and distribution. Even if a will includes a residuary clause, the testator could indicate that it was not his intention that the residue referred to all of his estate not specifically or generally described, such as certain property to be divided according to the statutory provision.

Whenever the testator provides for the distribution of much of his property among a number of beneficiaries, he may likewise mention specific items of ownership which will go to certain beneficiaries and general bequests and devises to others.

In many cases, the residue represents the major part of the estate. Special devises and bequests will often be designated; and following the payment of medical and hospital expenses incurred during the testator's last illness, the cost of administering the estate, plus the payment of all outstanding debts, and sometimes the payment of state and federal taxes, the residue of the estate will usually go to a particular beneficiary.

Consequences of Omissions

Should the draftsman's mistake involve a material part of the estate, such an act should not necessarily invalidate the entire content of the document in view of the fact that other provisions of the will would not be controlled or affected by the oversight. Neither could it be concluded that the mistake should represent conclusive evidence as to the testator's lack of understanding of other separate provisions of the will.

In a Kansas[1] decision, the court contended that the provisions of the will, as drafted, expressed the testator's desire; and, generally speaking, the conclusion was that a mistake of the draftsman was, nevertheless, binding on the testator. Likewise, an omission of terms of the will, such as the residuary clause, the amount of the legacy or bequest, or the names of devisees and legatees were considered mistakes of the testator and binding on him.

If it is so expressed in the testator's will that the child had been purposely omitted, no reason could be offered by the child to justify a protest. A parent is not legally responsible for mentioning a child in his will. Instead, there exists only a moral obligation toward including a child in the parent's will. The language might infer the intention of the testator to disqualify the child from sharing in the estate. However, in case the child is not mentioned, he might show cause for offering a protest on the ground of unintentional oversight.

Manner of Inheritance

As a rule, the testator will mention in his will whether his estate is to be divided among his children according to per capita (by the head) or per stirpes (by the number of fam-

[1] Hoover v. Roberts, 144 Kan 58, 58 P (2d) 83, 90, ALR (2d) 939 (1936).

ilies). An explicit designation is important so as to leave no doubt as to the intention of the testator. At the time of execution of the will, this question of distribution will necessarily be impressed on the testator's mind if he has children who might be of marriageable age or if the children are married. Otherwise, failure to include the possibility of future grandchildren might be attributed to an oversight. In the absence of the testator's referring to the interests of grandchildren, some statutes hold that the property shall be divided according to per capita, while other statutes observe the per stirpes principle. The latter rule appears to represent a favorable trend.

Statutes often provide that whenever a child is born subsequent to the execution of a will, either the entire will is revoked or the child is allowed to inherit under the law of descent and distribution. Should the terms of the will clearly indicate an intention on the part of the testator to disinherit an unborn child, the courts are in agreement that the birth of an after-born child does not revoke the will. Courts are divided on the procedure when nothing is said regarding an after-born child, with some courts contending that the will is revoked; while others holding that it is not affected by such an incident.

Frequently, confusion arises when a young married couple are enjoying the planning of a family and financial security, along with the acquiring of a house, furniture, automobile, boat, etc. Should the husband die prematurely without leaving a will, the young widow will be entitled only to her legal share, which usually amounts to about one-third, leaving the two-thirds to go to the children. When it becomes necessary to have the property sold, the Probate Court will have to be petitioned to appoint a guardian over the interests of the children. Disposing of the property is possible only with the consent of the court. Accordingly, confusion could be avoided thereafter by merely taking a little time in drafting a brief will leaving perhaps everything to his spouse in reliance on her good judgment in caring for the welfare of the children.

Use of "Devise" and "Bequest"

The terms legacy and bequest are used in referring to personal property in a will, but sometimes they ascribe to real property as well. The parties in a will who are to receive personal property are described as legatees. The term devise is used in a will in referring to real property to be transferred, although the term bequeath might be used as a synonymous expression. The more or less traditional approach in preparing a will is to set forth in the introduction the following expression: "Being of sound mind and disposing memory, I give, bequeath, and devise . . ." The word "give" could well signify all of the property passing under the will, including both real and personal property.

The testator has the responsibility of making bequeaths and devises crystal clear. Where designated and identifiable real or personal property is expressly referred to, there can be no cause for confusion. But where certain undivided property is left to more than one person, the time will come when the co-owners will deem it advisable to petition the Court of Equity for a partition of the property. If the will calls for the distribution of a farm, for example, containing a number of acres to more than one party, questions will have to be decided among the devisees as to the manner of division or else invoke the aid of the Equity Court.

Safeguard Against Vagueness

When a testator undertakes to write his own will, he is thereby placing himself in the position of a legal expert on the subject. What may seem to be a clear expression to the testator might possibly appear quite vague to a disinterested party. The basis of such misunderstanding sometimes can be attributed to the testator's failure to consider the difficulty of the Probate Court in concluding just what the testator meant.

As to the question of dealing with advancements which have been made to the testator's heirs, the draftsman of the will is justified in mentioning the amount which will be deducted from the share of the estate to which such heirs were entitled under the will. The deduction will be made even to the extent of the full amount, despite the errors in the advancement figures. In other words, whenever the amount to be deducted is clearly set forth, this figure cannot be offset even though questions are raised concerning mistakes attributed to the testator.

Courts have taken the position that it is the right of the testator to specify any amount which is intended to go to a beneficiary regardless of his reasoning in arriving at the particular conclusion. Actually, the testator is privileged to leave any discretionary portion of his estate, even nothing, to others. An exception, of course, is the right of a testator's spouse who possesses the legal right to take under the will or according to the legal statutory provision.

Chapter 7

Justifiable Cause for Revocation

When a testator drafts his will, he is giving an expression to his discretionary privilege. Thus, it emphasizes the freedom which he has exercised in indicating his personal wishes concerning his estate. It implies, also, that in the future, he has the authority to rescind that which he had previously declared. The obligation is unlike a contract between two parties whereby upon one's failure to perform, he will be liable for damages due to the inconvenience and expense which has been caused the other contracting party. Revocation of the will, moreover, can be made in various ways, such as destroying the instrument, mutilating, burning, erasing, or by writing the word revoked, canceled, void, annulled, or other similar words on the face of the instrument.

Anticipation of Change

When the testator prepares his will, it is usually the result of considerable meditation and possible assistance from someone who is familiar with the legal requirements of a will. Actually, what might be considered sound judgment by the testator at the time of the drafting of his will could very well become quite outmoded soon thereafter because of changes in the estate itself or possibly due to the testator's urge to make radical changes either in the beneficiaries or in the nature of the property intended for different parties.

Realizing the numerous circumstances which had influenced his moral obligation toward various beneficiaries, the testator becomes more alerted year after year to keep his will up-to-date in view of sudden changes which are constantly affecting his estate. To this end, he may wish to exercise his prerogative from time to time in the updating of the devises and bequests of his estate.

Effects of Irregularities

The testator's exercise of his discretionary right in drafting his will is not to be considered an obligatory act even though it might have been prepared subsequent to his making certain commitments having to do with the naming of beneficiaries. Assuming that illusory promises are purely gratuitous with nothing of value being transferred in the form of consideration given in exchange for the testator's promise to name a beneficiary as a legatee or devisee for designated property, nothing could prevent a revocation of the will at the testator's option. Conversely, when a beneficiary is described in the will as a legatee or devisee of certain property as a result of the testator's having received something of value in return for the definite promise set forth in the will, the acknowledged obligation is binding on the testator.

The existence of obvious irregularities in the testator's will might not result in its being invalidated, but, nevertheless, could easily give rise to those having vested interests in the estate to petition the Probate Court not to recognize the will for possessing probation quality. The testator is often inclined to use expressions in his will which are perfectly clear to him but at the same time suggest an element of vagueness to others. For instance, relatives might be referred to merely by their first names. Servants of the testator might also be mentioned by their first names, which could be very confusing years thereafter following the death of the testator.

The problem as to which party included in the execution of a will signed the document first and whether all parties signed in the presence of each other has caused no little amount of unnecessary trouble for the courts. Even a mark of identification can be used for a signature in many jurisdictions. Some authorities yet contend that a fingerprint or a thumbprint can be used when such name is not included in the body of the instrument.

A codicil is considered effective as an addition to the will or a deletion of provisions contained therein. When space is available on the original will itself, the codicil can be included with the document. Usually, however, it is prepared separately and is identified as representing a part of the will.

Reasonable Presumptions

Some jurisdictions contend that a will bearing a later date will have priority over a previously-drawn will even though the terms are not inconsistent with each other. The terms used either expressly or impliedly indicate an intention of the testator to revoke all previous wills. A former view of the courts was that a will bearing a later date did not in itself revoke a previous will bearing identical terms, and both could be presented for probation. This position involved unnecessary details. The modern view is that a will capable of being probated and bearing the most recent date will have priority.

Of course, there will be a tendency for every individual who has a vested interest in a will to interpret its content in the light of how his personal increment will be affected. Knowing full well these possibilities, the testator should endeavor to make the meaning of his will crystal clear, thus leaving nothing to the imagination to be implied. In the absence of the presence of the deceased at the time of probation of the will, specific inferences are apt to be made relative to the implications of certain written expressions.

At the death of an individual, particularly if he is possessed with considerable wealth, a question which is of great concern to interested parties is whether or not the deceased left a will. In the absence of its being presented for probation within a reasonable time after death, the only logical conclusion which could be drawn would be either no will existed or else it had been destroyed or misplaced. Meanwhile, a possibility could exist relative to someone who had knowledge of its whereabouts and who might have been responsible for its disappearance, particularly when his right to the estate, according to the law of descent and distribution, would be more than his share under the will itself. Recognizing the feasibility of such an irregularity, the testator should endeavor to protect the rights of acknowledged beneficiaries.

Contemplation of Impending Death

Having received definite warning that death is approaching, an owner of an estate places little value thereafter on his ownership for his own personal enjoyment; but a serious and conscientious person, under the circumstances, will be concerned about the future welfare of his dependents and very close relatives. Where there is absent any indication of interest expressed in planning for an eventual take-over of his possessions, he may prefer to follow the line of least resistance in doing nothing toward preparing a will, thereby leaving all property to be divided by operation of law. Whenever an important task of drafting a will is postponed until one receives a warning signal that death is near, interested parties in the estate will frequently lose little time after the testator's death in searching for justifiable reasons for challenging the will for probation on the possible grounds of incapacity of the testator or undue influence which had been exercised in causing him to act not in accordance with his personal convictions.

Generally speaking, the courts contend that the granting of a divorce does not in itself revoke the will of the testator or the testatrix as the case might be. In any event, if one's marital status has changed by a divorce decree, it would constitute an act of carelessness for anyone possessing a will not to take advantage of a number of ways of revoking it. In case death overtakes him before such a right is exercised, the granting of a divorce will not affect the will. Courts have held that where the divorce settlement in favor of the surviving spouse was less than the amount allowed under the law, the spouse was entitled to the difference.

Material Alteration

New wills can be made frequently if the testator so desires. Conditions may change in later years which will influence the testator to make corresponding changes in his will. Precaution must be taken not to create suspicion of fraud through erasures or in using some type of eradicator. Instead of endeavoring to make alterations consisting of additions to or deletions from the will, the purpose can be more safely accomplished by writing another will or in preparing a codicil which is also signed by the testator and properly attested.

The lapse of a long period of time following the preparing of a will might influence the testator to make alterations in the will and perhaps even revoke it altogether. Some units of property might have been either discarded or lowered in value. Meanwhile, the value of other units might have become greatly inflated. The testator has a responsibility of continually observing the various adjustments which should be made in his devises and bequests. As an equalizing measure, the testator sometimes is possessed with a strong urge to make certain alterations or additions by means of a codicil or in the drafting of a new will.

A holographic will, written in the testator's own handwriting, can be altered by the testator himself without destroying its validity, assuming that the testator was satisfied in having the alterations become a part of the will. However, the alterations made by someone other than the testator invalidates the will. Some courts have held that an attorney who made some corrections in the will while in the presence of the testator and with his knowledge and consent does not make the instrument unenforceable.

Additions and Deletions

Following the drafting of his will, the testator has a justifiable reason for desiring to be kept informed at all times concerning the actual content of his will, as well as the changing circumstances which could offer an inducement to the testator to alter certain provisions in his will. If the need for many changes appears obvious, conclusions might be safely drawn as to the advisability of his preparing a new will altogether. The terms of one's will involving a relatively small estate may remain quite satisfactory for a number of years provided it is brief and to the point with everything going, for instance, to the testator's spouse.

The problem becomes more complicated with the types of ownership being varied, and the beneficiaries being several in number. Assuming the possibility of a will to maintain its probation and distribution quality for a number of years, it is within the realm of probability that due to certain changes of conditions and circumstances, one's will can become quite deficient and unsatisfactory to the testator even soon after its drafting.

Upon recognizing the ineffectiveness of one's will, steps can immediately be taken to have it revoked. The simplest approach is to prepare another will which either expresses, or else implies, that the will revokes all previous wills made by the testator. Blacking out or marking through certain portions of a will would not necessarily revoke the entire will, but the procedure would be subject to considerable suspicion by the courts, as well as parties possessing vested interests in the estate. Naturally, a preferred and acceptable procedure for indicating such changes in bequests and devises is through the execution of a codicil with the same statutory formality as in the will itself. The codicil will usually be attached to the will or refer to it for conveying the intention of the testator to have the codicil supplement the provisions in the will. Even where a will has been revoked, a codicil can show the intention of the testator to have it revived.

Exercising Revocation Power

An instrument which is acceptable as a revocation of a previous will, whether it is a new and complete document or merely an addition to or a deletion from an existing will, the various states are quite uniform in requiring that in either case, it must include all of the formalities and requirements of a will. In the will containing the most recent date, emphasis should be given to such qualities as competency of parties, proper attestation, number of witnesses, and freedom from interference from others by way of fraud, duress, or undue influence. Should the later will fail to qualify for probation due to its defectiveness, the former will has been recognized by the courts as not having been revoked.

Since a will is not intended to become effective until the testator's death, the right to revoke is interpreted as being ever present. Unlike a living trust which could be declared irrevocable, the will does not become effective for probation so long as the testator is living. The various happenings could occur which would influence the testator to change his mind:

(a) Beneficiaries mentioned in a will are growing up, dying off, committing questionable acts of which the testator disapproves, or members of the family have increased or decreased in number.

(b) The estate has been in the process of change in view of some properties showing inflated values, while other properties have become deflated.

(c) Since preparing the will, the estate consists of after-acquired property, for which an allowance was not mentioned in the previous will.

(d) Subsequent to the drafting of a will, certain properties had been discarded, traded, or sold which would lead to confusion and disappointment in its distribution which, of course, could be avoided by way of constantly up-dating the previous will.

(e) Under the common law, married women were not favorites of the law. When a woman married, her will was revoked; but the law did not apply similarly to a man, since his will was not affected following his marriage. These inconsistencies have been superseded by statute in giving married women equal privileges with husbands, insofar as the making of a will is concerned. As a rule, the statutes of the various states regard the will of a husband or wife prepared before marriage as becoming revoked at the time of marriage. Specific exceptions are observed in antenuptial arrangements.

(f) The destruction, cancellation, or mutilation of a will results in its revocation; and the only alternative of the court is that the act represented the intention of the testator.

(g) Where there are births or legal adoptions, the courts insist on the child's receiving his share of the estate unless the testator's intention in his will clearly indicates otherwise.

Part II

Problems Encountered at Death

Chapter 8

Discovering Testator's Motives

Upon the death of the testator, it is oftentimes discovered that he had failed to make prominent in the minds of the readers of his last will and testament that which presumably was uppermost in his own mind. This becomes obvious to the court when endeavoring to analyze the vague and ambiguous statements. The simplest and most frequent-occurring request for the settlement of one's estate is for all of the debts of the deceased, the cost of administering the estate, and possibly taxes to be paid out of the residue, after which the net estate will be divided according to specific and general designations.

Significance of Devises and Bequeaths

Consideration is given by the court to every provision in the will, including the attached codicil. The conditions prevailing at the time of its execution will represent the basis for determing the testator's decisions. The court must endeavor to assume the position of the testator at the time the will was drafted in order to get a clear conception of the actual motives for the various provisions in his will.

Sometimes when a will is being probated, it is discovered that a legacy has been bequeathed to a beneficiary who was dead even at the time the will was drafted. Some courts contend that a testamentary gift is inapplicable to a dead person, and thus the legacy would be considered void. When the law does not provide that an issue of the beneficiary, who will share in such interest, no affirmative conclusion could be drawn. The court will not assume the responsibility of formulating rules relative to such technical and unusual situations. Wherefore, the court will not be disposed to gazing into the crystal ball for determining what should have been done by the testator or what might have been done. Instead, the court has to deal with the facts as they actually exist. Rather than endeavoring to make changes to fit more conveniently into a clearer pattern, the court must consider only the available written evidence.

While pondering over the testator's motives in certain instances, and, meanwhile, entertaining an awareness as to the right of every testator to designate how his estate will be divided, one can only imagine the confusion, under such conditions, which faces a conscientious court. Whenever one part of the will needs some clarification in the wording in order to make it consistent with other provisions, the court might include reasonable observations in the interest of promoting clearness of expression, rather than quite indifferently concluding that the will does not possess probation standards.

Congress has endeavored to let the various states decide whether or not the wife of the testator must share in the payment of the federal estate tax in the absence of any contrary specification by the testator. The court called attention to the Montana statute in not exempting the surviving spouse from sharing in the payment of the federal estate tax unless the testator had indicated otherwise.[1]

Circumstances Alter Cases

Even though the precedents of courts do not acknowledge devises and bequests in a testator's will unless the intention was unmistakably clear, exceptions to the general rule are sometimes deemed necessary. In an Ohio decision, a lady, whose brother was quite wealthy, spent many of her youthful years caring for her invalid mother. Her brother left all of his estate in his will to his spouse with a suggestion that she use her own discretion in looking after the needs of his sister. The court ruled in favor of the sister of the deceased by way of declaring that the size of the estate justified an exception to the rule of requiring that expressions used in making a testamentary disposition of his estate must be reasonably clear and definite.

Courts have recognized wills executed by individuals while under the influence of alcohol provided the facts revealed the testators' adequate knowledge of their actions. Merely offering evidence to support the contention that a testator was an alcoholic would not justify the court's refusing to allow a testator's will to be probated.

[1] Robinson v. United States, 369 F Supp 925 (1974).

Indefinite Expressions

In endeavoring to interpret the expressions of a testator in an effort to discover just what was meant by the written word, the courts frequently recognize the testator's chief concern in promoting harmony among those to whom his property will be mainly entrusted; namely, his spouse and children. This frequently accounts for the testator's using expressions which are quite vague, including: "hope," "wish," "trust," and "discretion." As a rule, the courts contend that unless a bequest clearly identifies the legatee, as well as the property, the court will feel justified in refusing to recognize the transfer. The court does not have the authority to substitute expressions for those made by the testator. Instead, an effort must be made to determine from the evidence the exact wishes of the testator.

Should a named beneficiary die before the execution of the will or died following the drafting of the will, such a devise or bequest normally would be considered void and unenforceable. However, circumstances could indicate that the property was intended for some other person. Had a child been living at the time of the testator's death, the implication might have been that the property was intended for such person. In a California[2] decision, the testator made a bequest to an organization by the name of "The Woman's Christian Temperance Union of Los Angeles." Three organizations with names similar claimed the bequest. The party who was responsible for the drafting of the will testified as to the testator's uncertainty of the actual name of the organization for which the bequest was intended; but the organization was described to the scribner who, in turn, telephoned the organization only to be given the incorrect name. The court declared that the organization for which the legacy was intended could be ascertained from the testimony of the scribner, and, therefore, allowed the name to be changed to "The Woman's Christian Temperance Union of Southern California."

Meaning of Children

In a Wisconsin[3] court decision, the residuary of the estate was left to "my children." Actually, some of the testator's children were adopted, while some of them were his own. The trial court held that the expression "my children" was ambiguous and did not include the "adopted children." When the decision was appealed to the Supreme Court, the precedent established

---

[2] In Re Little, 170 Cal. 52, 148 p 194, 90 ALR 2d 955 (1915).

[3] Re Estate of McDonald, 20 Wis 2d 63, 121 NW 2d 245, 96 ALR 2d 634 (1963).

was that the term "children," insofar as the inheritance was concerned, included "adopted children" and reversed the state court decision in maintaining that the lower court had erred in excluding the evidence for determining the testator's intention.

According to the English Common Law, an illegitimate child could inherit from nobody. Statutes have been amended giving the right to such a person to inherit from his mother, but silent as to the right to inherit from his mother's ancestors. In the absence of any statutory provision, an illegitimate child possesses no right of inheritance from his mother's relatives.

Advances to Children

When a transfer of property is made by a testator to a legatee or devisee, it is not to be inferred that the gift is to be considered as a redemption to be deducted from the donee's share of his bequest in the will. Neither should any advances made by the testator prior to the execution of his will be subjected to redemption unless the testator mentions in his will that gifts to one's children represent advances which will be considered as such insofar as deductions are concerned.

An often-quoted expression concerning a will is that "it speaks as of the death of the testator." If any debts to which the testator has a claim are to be released, special attention should be called to them. In a Kentucky[4] decision, the father had lived with his son for more than twenty years. The son had borrowed money from his father. On different occasions, the son had offered to pay off the debt, but the father refused claiming that he would make an allowance for the debt in his will. The court contended that the testator had indicated an intention to release his son from his debt.

Conditional Bequests and Devises

In order to give assurance that the testator's wishes will be enforced according to his particular dictation as set forth in his will, it is sometimes stipulated that anyone who endeavors to contest the will thereby surrenders and forfeits any interest which he might have in the estate. This is to prevent any interested party from contesting the will on the grounds of fraud,

---

[4] May v. Williams, 208 Ky 232, 270 SW 804 (1925).

duress, mistake, or undue influence. Some courts do not look with favor on this type of procedure on the theory of its being against the interest of public policy in depriving a beneficiary of his privilege of promoting justice and fair play when it appears obvious that certain factors influenced the testator to act in such a manner not consistent with his better judgment.

A testator sometimes mentions in his will that certain property will go to a designated legatee or devisee provided he or she has a child. Whether an adopted child will fulfill this requirement is a question requiring the attention of the court. Whenever an inheritance is concerned, the adoption of a child would appear to meet this condition. The court decisions, moreover, have indicated a different viewpoint in maintaining that an adopted child fails to satisfy the condition specifically set forth in the will. The expression used in the testator's will would imply, it seems, that he was quite concerned with having a bodily heir of his son to inherit his estate rather than have it subsequently inherited by someone possessing no blood relationship.

Influence of Marriages and Births

Statutes vary as to the tendency which a marriage or the birth of a child following one's drafting of a will might have on its effectiveness. In the states which hold that either of the two events will revoke the will, a distinction is made between the births of a legitimate and an illegitimate child. In the latter, the will of the father would not be affected since the illegitimate child could not inherit from him unless he subsequently recognized in writing the child as being his own, in which case the child would inherit a child's part in the absence of a will. Thus, the will quite naturally would become ineffective. Should the child later become legitimatized by marriage of parents, the previous will would likewise be revoked.

Some states distinguish between a living child at the time of the drafting of the will and an after-born child. There is no legal obligation of a parent to include a child in his will; but as to the after-born child, it is implied that the parent entertained an intention to include him. Hence, he would be entitled to inherit a child's part under the law of descent and distribution. Should a parent wish to exclude an after-born child, in the event such a child was subsequently born, from sharing in his estate, the will could very well express this intention. The *Ohio Revised Code* endeavors to protect the spouse in the case of an after-born child in allowing such a child an intestate share "to the portion of the estate not devised or bequeathed to or for the use of the surviving spouse."

As to the parents' responsibility for the care of their children, some courts hold that failure to mention children in the will is equivalent to the parents' dying intestate and entitling the children to share according to the law of descent and distribution. Other states hold that the omissions of children in the parents' will could be parallel to their not leaving a will unless it appeared obvious that the omissions were intentional. It can be expressed in the will that the children are not included in the inheritance, and it could be mentioned also that this exclusion applied as well to any after-born children.

Significance of Residue

The testator often observes a customary pattern of designating a few small bequests to various parties but leaving the bulk of his estate in the residue to be distributed according to some general plan. For instance, a husband may mention devisees and legatees who will receive minor portions of the estate but leaving the major part to his spouse with complete confidence in her capacity and good judgment of caring for it. This would amount to the residue being left to the survivor as representing the larger share. In the event the testator had no bodily heirs, the property left in his will to his spouse should, at least, approximate the amount to which she would be entitled by law.

An ambiguity, no doubt, would be created should the testator merely state that the residue of his estate was to be distributed to designated parties without any explanation as to the manner of procedure. The question as to the ratio or percentage to be observed might result in confusion. Such a vague expression would not indicate whether the testator's intention was to divide the residue equally or to give priority of right to certain beneficiaries with the remainder, if any, to be divided among secondary parties. Conversely, mentioning a number of legatees, each of whom is to receive an equal share of the estate, could create no misunderstanding in regard to the intention of the testator.

When certain property is definitely designated in the testator's will to go to particular legatees or devisees, and one or more of such parties dies before the death of the testator, the property ordinarily will become a part of the residue, resulting in portions of the estate going to those sharing in the residue unless it is stipulated that the share of the deceased will go to another described beneficiary. Likewise, if a testamentary gift represents a special devise or bequest and the property is sold or discarded prior to the death of the testator, such a special designation will, of course, lapse.

Chapter 9

Probation Consideration

Prior to a court decision recognizing a will for probation, the Probate Court will inquire into the legal aspects of the document, as well as the conditions under which it was prepared. Sometimes a very crudely-written will may be allowed for probation when the court is convinced that the document sufficiently expresses the intention of the testator and represents his last will and testament. Furthermore, the court desires to have complete and definite assurance that the will was not the result of undue influence having been exercised over the testator.

Custodian of the Will

Just where the will was located at the time of its discovery, following the death of the testator, may not appear to the ordinary layman as being very significant. Yet, some courts emphasize the importance of its being included among the testator's business papers in order to refute the possibility of someone's having purposely and intentionally caused it to become pigeonholed in some irregular and inconspicuous place.

For convenience, and also for safety reasons, the testator in some jurisdictions is permitted to file his will with the Probate Court for a small fee and, in turn, secure a receipt. The name of the testator on the wrapper, which carries the signature of the Probate Court, will constitute identification. Upon request, the party whose name appears on the wrapper will be entitled to have a return of the will at his discretion. Also, the party to whom the will should be transferred at the death of the testator, who is usually the executor, will be entitled to its receipt at the proper time.

In the event the name of the transferee is not mentioned on the wrapper, the court must exercise his duty in removing the wrapper to discover the proper person to whom it should be delivered for presentment to be probated. The difficulty of entrusting the will to the custody of the court is in the event the testator desires to revoke, change, or alter the instrument, it will necessitate his having to request of the Probate Court its return. Naturally, a plan more convenient for the testator is to keep his will in his safety deposit box at his own local bank rather than to entrust it to the custody of the court.

The one in possession of the will of the deceased is responsible for offering it for probation as soon as possible following the testator's death. Some states impose a penalty against one in possession of the will who fails to offer it for probation within the statutory time limit. This would involve, to be sure, one's having knowledge of its location or with the exercise of reasonable diligence he could have discovered it. For example, had a person been informed as to his nomination in the testator's will as executor, he certainly would be alerted in endeavoring to locate the will. In like manner, if a known trustee in the will entertains some suspicion that someone was purposely withholding the will without revealing its location, he, too, would feel duty bound to petition the court to compel the custodian to offer the will for probation.

The Probate Court recognizes the right of any individual having a vested interest in the estate of the deceased to offer it for probation. It often happens that when a husband dies, only his surviving spouse will have knowledge concerning the whereabouts of her husband's will. As a rule, the executor will be the logical person for presenting the will for probation, and the one in possession of the will usually displays an attitude of wholehearted cooperation in gladly surrendering it to the executor immediately after the death of the testator. Under such circumstances, in the event the one in possession of the will refuses to surrender it, the Probate Court will have no other alternative than to issue an order to the party withholding the instrument to surrender it within a designated period of time. In case such a party fails to observe the court's order, he or she will become subject to a penalty which might well include an imprisonment until the will is surrendered.

Court of Probation

The will must be filed in the office of the Probate Court in the county in which the deceased claimed as his place of domicile. While the filing of the will for probation is usually associated with the duties of the executor, anyone in possession of the will can be expected to surrender it to the court or else to the executor. Sometimes the will is entrusted to an attorney, in which case, he will be responsible for its filing. Some parties are quite partial toward leaving all of their testamentary documents in the possession of attorneys who are trained in legal requirements and procedures.

In certain jurisdictions, the executor is compelled to employ an attorney for filing the will for probation, particularly whenever there are beneficiaries other than the executor or executrix. Beneficiaries may wish to keep the cost of administration of the estate to a minimum while expecting the executor to perform the necessary legal duties, for which he may not be qualified, without the assistance of legal counsel. Of course, the executor cannot use the Probate Court as a crutch for informing him as to how he should proceed. It must be understood by the executor that the responsibility of the court is not to instruct the executor concerning what steps should be taken when presenting the will for probation, in the absence of the testator's possessing any knowledge relative to the proper legal requirements involved.

When the services of others are employed, the executor is entitled to protect the estate from any overcharge. To avoid any such misunderstanding and dissatisfaction resulting from seemingly excessive fees, an agreement beforehand could be entered into relative to the approximate charge that will be made for the particular services. This could be a means of avoiding the inconvenience and expense of possibly having to later petition the court for a ruling concerning what should represent a reasonable fee, under the circumstances. Should there exist a situation between husband and wife of absolute trust and confidence in each other, it is a feasible plan for them to arrange their property ownership to be held in joint tenancy with the right of survivorship as a means of escaping the expense and inconvenience in having a will probated.

Quality of Will for Probation

Determining the necessary quality of a will to insure its probation is a problem for the Probate Court to decide. It is not for the court to conclude whether or not the testator acted wisely in naming certain legatees and devisees. The main concern of the court is to conclude if the document possessed all of the legal requirements for probation. The court, therefore, will be guided by the facts contained in the will itself, in the absence of an issue raised by an interested party regarding certain irregularities contained therein. Even though a testator is incapable of signing his name to his will, courts maintain that this deficiency should not deprive him of his privilege of having his estate distributed at his death according to his dictation. Rather, his signature, which might be expressed by a mere mark, would be legal, assuming the attesting witnesses were qualified and the will in every other way was regular and valid.

The law recognizes the right of a testator to exclude from his last will and testament any individual, other than one's spouse, from sharing in his estate following his death. Such intention can be expressed in no uncertain terms that the particular heir will receive only certain property with no further expectation of his receiving anything in addition. Should nothing be stated concerning the residue of the estate, courts have observed the procedure of allowing the distribution of the residue according to the law of descent and distribution.

As a general rule, a will cannot be probated until it is properly presented for that purpose after the testator's death. However, courts have made exceptions in cases where the will had been destroyed, without the testator's knowledge, prior to his death. Should the evidence convince the court that the will had been lost before the testator's death without his cognizance, the court, nevertheless, may allow such facts, under unusual circumstances, to constitute the last will and testament and possessing the necessary probation quality.

Filing for Probation

Every state has a statute of limitations for presenting a will for probation. The State of Arkansas[1] has a prohibitory law

1 Sims v. Schaney, 351 SW 2d 145, 87 ALR 2d 718 (1961).

forbidding the offering of a will for probation after five years following the death of the testator. Yet, the statute was silent as to the time for presenting a foreign will which had been probated in Louisiana, the testator's place of domicile. The court held that since the will had already been probated in a foreign state, the time of probation in Arkansas would not be barred by the Arkansas Statute of Limitations.

State statutes endeavor to promote vigilance on the part of the person in possession of the will of the deceased to present it for probation within a reasonable time. Usually, the statute is very specific as to this question and prescribes a severe penalty for failure to fulfill the requirements. In a very early Ohio[2] decision, the court held that a beneficiary who had knowledge as to the existence of such a will and failed to have it presented for probation within three years would lose his right to any lands, tenements, or hereditaments, and, as a result, that portion of the estate would descend to those recognized as the heirs of the testator.

Determining Validity of Will

It is not necessary that the property which is mentioned in a will is given in contemplation of imminent death. Statutes define contemplation of death as a natural occurrence which influences an individual to draft a will as a means of preparing for an orderly transfer of his property after his death. A will often recites that the testator signed the will in the presence of the witnesses which merely amounts to an acknowledgment of the testator's signature and not the will itself. In the event the statute governing wills requires its publication, the testator must reveal that the instrument was the testator's last will and testament.

Should a beneficiary be mentioned in the will as a devisee or a legatee, he would not be qualified to witness the signing of the will in case the establishment of its validity depended on his attesting capacity. Thus, his rights under the will would be declared void, after which the witness would be recognized as competent to testify concerning the execution of the will.

Non-attesting witnesses can offer evidence for establishing the validity or the invalidity of the will. The mental capacity of

2 Carpenter v. Denoon, 29 OS 379 (1876).

the testator at the time of executing his will would be of great importance to the court. Furthermore, such a witness might be able to contribute to the legality or the illegality of the will in testifying as to the conditions under which the will was executed—that is, whether the will was a result of fraud, misrepresentation, duress, or undue influence.

Acceptance or Non-Acceptance

A testator is expected to possess a sound mind and disposing memory in order to qualify as being sufficiently competent to make a will. A test of one's capacity to make a will is knowledge as to the extent of his ownership and his indicating a definite and accurate pattern of bequests and devises of his estate. The law does not disqualify one for making a will purely on the basis of age or physical ailments. Rather, an aged person should be encouraged to draft his will if it is not coupled with fraud or influence unduly exercised by interested parties. If questions as to the shortcomings of an aged person, such as failing memory, are raised, courts will be inclined to look with caution and suspicion on the testator's testamentary capacity to make a will.

It is quite probable that following the death of the testator, other wills bearing varied dates may be offered for probation. Usually the motive for preparing more than one will at different times is due to changes in beneficiaries, the estate itself constantly undergoing changes, and the inflated and deflated values of certain devises and bequests. The mere misplacing of a will may result in the drafting of another. Even though the death of an attesting witness would not make the instrument void, the testator would certainly be on the safe side in preparing a new will. Where more than one will is offered for probation, the one bearing the latest date will, of course, receive priority by the court. It is obvious that the will may not be accepted for probation if it is too indefinite. In case a part of the will is deemed invalid as a result of mistake, fraud, or undue influence while the other part is valid, the court will ordinarily recognize that part which is legal provided it is clearly distinguishable.

Confirmation of Executor's Nomination

Merely mentioning in a will the name of the executor who will execute the wishes of the testator gives no absolute assurance that the nomination will meet with the court's approval for various reasons:

(a) Objections offered by beneficiaries.
(b) Immaturity as to age and experience.
(c) Failing health.
(d) Inactivity due to old age.
(e) Lacking proper maturity of judgment.
(f) Frequent absences from the state.
(g) Charges of improper conduct.
(h) Reputation for dishonesty.
(i) Crime recently committed.
(j) Indifference as to general attitude.

As a rule, the court will have little or no justification for failing to confirm the wishes of the testator's nomination of the executor unless the beneficiaries offer the above-mentioned objections for disqualifying such a fiduciary. Should the testator's nomination of the executor be confirmed, the court will issue a letter of testamentary to the executor. A letter of administration is issued when an administrator is appointed by the court.

Chapter 10

Priorities of Surviving Spouse

When the will clearly identifies the beneficiaries, including the surviving spouse, there can be no questions raised with respect to the intention of the testator, particularly when those who are mentioned are identically the parties to whom the property would go under the legal principle of descent and distribution. Heirs at law represent those who would be entitled to the estate in case the owner should die intestate. In the event the testator was indefinite in referring to his heirs as the beneficiaries, the court in some situations might be left with no other alternative than to apply the statute.

Right of Reimbursement

The funeral costs, as well as the expenses incurred during the last illness of the deceased, are sometimes quite large. Wherefore, the surviving spouse will be justified in carefully examining the will of the deceased to discover whether or not provisions have been made for taking care of necessary expenditures rather than having such burden imposed on the survivor. Where controls and limitations are not observed in the funeral arrangements, thus permitting the undertaker to largely exercise his own discretion in this matter, the expense incurred can become unreasonably large. As a general rule, funeral expenses are recognized for receiving priority in the payment of obligations of the deceased.

According to an early Kentucky[1] court decision, a husband

[1] In Ketterer v. Nelson, 146 Ky 7, 141, SW 409, 37 LRA NS 754 (1911).

sought a refund from his deceased wife's estate to the extent of her last illness and funeral expenses. A reimbursement to the extent of the last illness, including the fees for nursing, the physician, and burial expenses, were not allowed by the court on the theory that they represented necessaries for the wife for which the husband was responsible. However, the court recognized the responsibility of the estate for such costs should the husband fail to pay.

In a similar Nebraska[2] case having to do with the responsibility of the husband for the last illness and the funeral expense of a husband's deceased wife, the court cited the common law which made the liability of the husband mandatory. The court contended that this is yet the prevailing view unless the statute decides otherwise. Thus, a reimbursement for the last illness and the funeral expenses of his deceased wife was denied.

The common law provision that a surviving spouse is responsible for the expenses incurred by the deceased husband or wife during his or her last illness is being altered in some states by way of allowing the surviving spouse such reimbursement. The *Ohio Revised Code*, Section 2117.26, provides some relief, with conditions, for the survivor: "The surviving spouse, whether husband or wife, is entitled to reimbursement for the funeral expenses of the deceased spouse if the expenses were paid by the surviving spouse to the extent that the rights of other creditors will not be prejudiced."

Widow's Allowance

During the time a will is being probated (which might be very brief or in some cases requiring a year or longer depending on the amount of the estate, the number of beneficiaries, and the nature of the property involved), one of the first requests of the attorney or executor to the court is that of seeking an allowance for the surviving widow and children (if any) which will be adequate for a year's expenditures. In some statutes, such an allowance is adequately provided for. In the state of Georgia,[3] a widow was allowed enough of the estate to assure her support for a year, and the marital deduction was allowed for this amount. A contrary view, however, was later

[2] Re White's Estate, 150 Neb 167, 33 NW (2d) 470 (1948).

[3] First National Bank & Trust Co. of Augusta v. United States, 191 F Supp 446, (DC-Ga) (1960).

taken by a Missouri[4] court in claiming that the allowance made to a widow did not amount to a terminable interest which will qualify for a marital deduction.

In determining the amount provided in the statute for the widow's allowance during the probation of the will, the law usually takes into consideration the needs of the widow, her social position, standard of living to which she has been accustomed, the size of the estate, the physical conditions of the widow, her age at the time, and the number of children (also their ages) for arriving at an allowance figure.

Right of Contest

Prior to the decision of the Probate Court to recognize the will for probation, notices must be served on the surviving spouse, and, in addition, those who are entitled to share in the estate of the deceased. In the absence of any testamentary provisions having been made, the surviving spouse cannot be deprived of his or her pecuniary interest in the estate. Many situations can exist which tend to give rise to a right of the survivor to contest the will. A surviving spouse in the state of Tennessee[5] would have been entitled to the personalty amounting to $18,-000 had the testatrix died intestate, while under the will, he was to receive only $2,000. Naturally, his interest was that of taking under the law.

While the court in Georgia[6] passed favorably on the nomination of the widow as executrix of her husband's estate, it was contended that her right to contest the will could not be denied unless other beneficiaries within a reasonable period of time could show cause why the will should not be set aside because of testamentary incapacity and other reasons. The various legatees alleged that the surviving spouse, having qualified as executrix, amounted to an estoppel in denying the validity of the will. The court held that the act of the executrix was not conclusive as to admission of the will for probation. The fact that the widow had agreed in writing to the probation of her husband's will did not estop her from exercising her right to contest the probation of the will.

[4] Phillips v. Bookwalter, (DC-Mo) 210 F Supp 801 (1962).
[5] Melody v. Hamblin, 21 Tenn AOO 687, 115 SW 2d 237x (1937).
[6] Gaither v. Gaither, 23 Ga 521, 78 ALR 2d 1072 (1857).

Right of Election

It is not obligatory that the devisee or legatee accept the transfer of property as provided in the will. A rejection might be expressed by a formal refusal in writing or by one's action. The surviving spouse, therefore, has the option of electing to take either under the will or by law. Should she decide to renounce her right under the will, in the absence of a statutory period during which she must make this election, the court will consider what would be a reasonable length of time for revoking her rights as set forth in the will of her deceased husband.

Because of a widow's deciding to take against the will in the state of Maryland,[7] the estate became considerably reduced in view of the large amount which had to be applied toward the payment of federal estate taxes, since the marital deduction was not being allowed. The court contended that the widow's share of the estate was to be determined after the payment of the federal estate tax. Consequently, the marital deduction was allowed under the Revenue Act for calculating the federal estate tax in order to provide adequate advantages similar to those enjoyed by others living in community property states.

The election of a widow in Kansas[8] to take under the law for receiving her share of her husband's estate, which was in excess of four million dollars, resulted in her share amounting to more than two million dollars, less $410,000 assessment for one-half of the federal estate tax burden. Under the circumstances, the court ruled that the widow's share of the estate was not to be diminished by the federal estate tax imposed against the estate of the deceased.

Descent and Distribution

When one dies intestate, his ownership will go to his successors by operation of law as defined in the particular state. Failure to mention devisees and legatees is frequently the result of negligence or procrastination. At the same time, there might be selfish motives for one's failure to designate his successors. A husband, for example, may not care to leave everything to his wife in accordance, perhaps, with her wishes. Also,

[7] Weinberg v. Safe Deposit & Trust Company of Baltimore, 198 Md 539, 85 A 2d 50, 37 ALR 2d 188 (1951).

[8] Sperrier, Appellant v. First Nat'l Bank of Wichita, Appellee 485 P 2d 209 (1971).

there may be beneficiaries who would share alike under the principle of descent and distribution, and this procedure might well be preferred by the testator, since the naming of beneficiaries could possibly result in jealousies and discontent among certain parties having vested interest in the estate.

When the owner of an estate dies without leaving a will, the law will prevail in determining those who should be included as heirs, the extent of ownership to which each heir is entitled, as well as priorities, if any, which might be allowed. The statute particularly regulates the rights of parties, such as the surviving spouse, children (including legitimate, illegitimate, and adopted), and also the heirs of the children of the deceased. If the deceased is not survived by a spouse or children, the law of descent and distribution will comprise relatives, according to statutory provisions, including parents, brothers, sisters, grandparents, uncles, nieces, cousins, etc.

In the absence of the drafting of a will by husband and wife and both should die simultaneously as a result of a single disaster, such as an automobile accident, an airplane crash, fire, cyclone, or the sinking of a ship, a complicated problem arises in determining which spouse deceased first in order to trace the line of inheritance. Even though one spouse survived the other, for only a very brief period, the law of inheritance by descent and distribution will apply. Thus, the surviving spouse will be entitled to his or her share of the estate of the predeceased spouse; and, in turn, the estate of the surviving spouse will be divided among his or her heirs at law.

Chapter 11

Rights and Duties of Beneficiaries

There exists during the lifetime of the testator only an expectancy of title to certain property by legatees and devisees who are the named beneficiaries in the will. Of course, nothing is definite or certain as to the eventual transferring of ownership as planned due to the testator's privilege and discretion of changing, altering, or revoking his will while he is living. Furthermore, the possibility that the property described in the will may be discarded, sold, or transferred by way of a gift or dedication cannot be overlooked. Then, too, an allowance must be made for the risk of ownership being surrendered involuntarily by a judicial sale or a trustee in bankruptcy. The title to the estate will vest in the devisees and legatees only after the probation of the will.

Discretionary Rights of Beneficiaries

As a general rule, when one is contemplating making a will, he considers the undertaking as representing his legal right and an individual privilege as well. Actually, he may not be possessed with any inclination of seeking the advice of beneficiaries. When the will calls for certain property to be sold and the proceeds to be divided among designated beneficiaries, the court will be guided by the wishes of the beneficiaries as to whether it would be advisable to have the property sold or else divided among those who have vested interests. The main consideration of the court is to have all parties concerned in the transfer to mutually agree to any proposed plan of distribution.

As to the rights of the beneficiaries to enter into an agreement prior to or subsequent to the testator's death in designating changes in the devises or bequests, courts are not in complete agreement concerning the rights of beneficiaries to deviate from the testator's directives. Some authorities insist on the transfers being made in accordance with the provisions in the will itself. However, any substitutions or deviations made by beneficiaries following the probation of the will is of no concern of the court.

Decisions as to Inheritances

In situations involving members of the family who agree to the distribution of the estate differently from that which is set out in the will, problems have arisen as to whether or not it mattered particularly if such agreements were entered into prior to the testator's death or following his death. When members of the family agree among themselves regarding what they deem to be an equitable settlement, courts, as a rule, will not intervene. While the courts recognize the rights of legatees to make settlements with one or more of the beneficiaries in a will, it does not imply that they must make agreements and compromises with others.

The general rule is that whenever a beneficiary is not altogether pleased with his share of the estate left him, he can agree with other beneficiaries to make exchanges. So long as beneficiaries can realize greater satisfaction and contentment through such a procedure, the court will usually acquiesce in order to avoid subsequent discontent and possible court litigation. Particularly where wills have been lost or destroyed, the law is sympathetic toward members of a family who are in agreement with regard to the manner of settlement.

Agreements With Beneficiaries

A promise of a beneficiary to pay a next of kin a certain sum of money provided such party agrees not to object to the probation of a will and accept the settlement without contest has met the approval of courts. On the other hand, when the promisee had no interest in the estate of the deceased, the promise of the beneficiary would be recognized as being illegal and in violation of public policy.

The courts are divided on the question of a beneficiary's

denouncing his right in a testamentary instrument despite the fact that he is obligated to the creditors of the deceased. While it is generally held that he has a right to do so, yet if his objective in declaring his renunciation is to defeat the claims of creditors, the courts have held an act of this type to be invalid. Of course, it would represent a very unusual occasion for a beneficiary to refuse a legacy or a devise mentioned in the testator's will. At the same time, the law does not make it mandatory for the acceptance of a testator's gift. Instead, courts have considered it optional with the legatees or devisees to accept or reject the gifts regardless of the value of the property involved.

In the event of a breach of contract between a legatee or devisee and the testator which is not discovered until after the death of the testator when the will is offered for probation and the facts are made available, the beneficiary will be entitled to a cause of action. In maintaining his right of indemnity against the estate of the deceased for breach of contract, the action must be brought against the legal representative.

Sharing of Losses

When the various expenses, including taxes, debts, funeral expenses, and cost of administration, are to be paid out of the residue of the estate, the testator is likely to reason that such a fund might possibly be insufficient for meeting all demands on the estate before the legatees and devisees are satisfied. It is possible that the testator will request that the expenses over and above the residue of the estate must be paid proportionately out of the shares of all beneficiaries after the payment in full to the designated legatees and devisees.

The testator has the discretion of making an allowance for the possibility of his estate having to meet unforeseen costs prior to his death, including medical bills, operation, hospitalization, and drugs, in addition to the loss of income for a long period of time from one's employment, business, or profession. Furthermore, there will be the cost of the executor, possibly a trustee, perhaps attorney fees, and court costs. An allowance cannot be overlooked for offsetting the costs resulting from delays, inconveniences, and confusion for the testator's immediate family in making the necessary adjustments in compliance with all legal requirements for the liquidation of an estate.

Unexpected Disadvantages

The often-quoted expression: "What was once nailed down is now coming apart" is invariably true in the case of an individual with dependents who dies prematurely and unexpectedly without having carefully pre-planned his future estate. The sudden transition, often accompanied with varied hardships, usually finds the surviving spouse poorly prepared and pitifully uninformed concerning the difficult problems to be encountered in the settling of the estate, including:

(a) The bank account of the deceased will be closed at the time of death.

(b) The safety deposit box at the bank becomes sealed and cannot be reopened until a representative from the tax office is able to take inventory of its content.

(c) The petitioning of the court for an advancement of a particular amount from the estate equivalent to the needs of the surviving spouse and children for usually a year.

(d) The petitioning of the Probate Court for the probation of the will (if any); otherwise, request the appointment of an administrator.

(e) Experiencing the possible delay in the probation of the will because of the petition filed by one or more of the interested parties as a protest to the probation of the will.

(f) The consideration given by the Probate Court to the matter of confirming the nomination of the executor.

(g) Expenses incurred in liquidating the estate.

(h) The estate becomes diminished as a result of the payment of inheritance tax and possibly federal estate tax.

(i) Expenditures for court costs and the administering of the estate.

(j) When a business is involved and provisions are made for its continued operation, certain disadvantages must be anticipated when there is to be a continued operation: (1) the risk of exploitation by the executor or trustee; (2) the disposing of the business in the future at an inopportune time; (3) inefficiency in management; (4) the trust arrangement giving too much discretionary authority to the trustees.

Proceeds from Liquidation

Following the executor's assuming control over the estate, his decision-making authority might be regulated according to specific provisions in the will. Sometimes the testator indicates complete confidence in the executor by way of granting him full discretion in disposing of certain property which, according to his opinion, represents the best time for endeavoring to make the transfer. Particularly, when real property or a profitable business is involved, greater returns can usually be anticipated for the beneficiaries provided the executor is allowed to retain the real property or to continue the operation of the business until he considers the time to be most opportune and profitable for negotiating a sale.

Generally, an estate can be liquidated and the proceeds prorated in one-year's time, or less, especially when the entire estate is left to the surviving spouse under the principle of joint tenancy with the right of survivorship. Conversely, when the estate is large and broad discretionary authority is granted the executor for awaiting the most suitable time for making transfers rather than having to do so as quickly as possible, the time involved for liquidating such an estate could very well extend over a period of time considerably longer than a year. Sometimes beneficiaries are uninformed and unsympathetic toward the many details involved in liquidating an involved estate and possibly will become quite impatient with the seemingly slow progress of the executor. This attitude on the part of some beneficiaries could lead to their exercising the privilege of petitioning the Probate Court either to pressure the executor for a speedier settlement of the estate or else to request his removal on the grounds of inefficiency.

Bequests and Devises

A general principle of law concerning the identification of real and personal property, insofar as the liquidation of an estate is concerned, is that the real property goes directly to the heirs at law, while the personal property passes to the legal representative, who is the executor or administrator. The difficulty in many instances comes in accurately classifying the property.

A testator in the state of Kansas[1] bequeathed in his will to his wife "the use of all my property, both real and personal, as to the rents, issues, profits, and proceeds thereof." The contention of the wife was that the wheat represented returns from rents and thus belonged to her. The court, in ruling otherwise, contended that the wheat being consumable did not fall within the category of rents which would accrue to the widow.

Circumstances alter cases, and one must always keep in mind that the law is what the courts determine the law is. The facts in a Michigan[2] case revealed that the testator's will provided for the devise of land on which wheat was growing at the time of the testator's death. The question arose in the probation of the will as to whether the wheat was personal property and should go to the executor or whether it was to be classed as a part of the realty which would rightly go to the devisees of the land. The court reasoned that even though a statute provided for the executor or administrator's receiving rents and profits from the estate, in this particular instance the executor possessed sufficient property for paying all claims against the estate. Hence, there was no necessity for the executor to apply the growing wheat toward the payment of debts of the estate or for the expense of administration.

In a North Carolina[3] issue, the reasoning of the court concerning growing crops was in keeping with the testator's clear directive about which there could be no misunderstanding. In the testator's will, he devised to his spouse his farm, including all growing crops. Meanwhile, a statute provided that growing crops would go to the executor at the testator's death. The court, nevertheless, contended that the crops belonged to the widow even though the statute provided otherwise.

A testator in Kentucky[4] was quite indefinite, claimed the court, in devising a life estate in all of his property to his wife. The question was whether the life estate provision in the testator's will included the right of the widow to use the corn growing on the farm toward feeding the livestock without hav-

[1] Re Blakely's Estate, 115 Kan 644, 224 P 65, 92 ALR 2d 1384 (1924).

[2] Rough v. Womer, 375 Mich 375, 403 NW 573, 92 ALR 2d 1384 (1889).

[3] Thomas v. Lines, 83 NC 191, 92 ALR 2d 1383 (1880).

[4] Miller v. Miller, 310 Ky 721, 221 SW 2d 654, 92 ALR 2d 1384 (1949).

ing to account to the remainderman. The state statute declared growing crops to be personalty which were to be applied toward the payment of debts and the expenses of administering the estate. The court further reasoned that since the payment of debts and the cost of administration had already been provided for, the court ruled that the growing crops in the particular case should be distributed according to the provisions in the testator's will.

As to the natural crops which do not come about as a result of cultivation by man, it is the general rule that such property necessarily goes with the land. Therefore, land that is devised in a testamentary disposition will also include the natural crops which are described in legal terminology, "fructus naturales."

Chapter 12

Filing Claims Against the Estate

The problems of the court are somewhat that of a mind reader in determining what the testator's wishes were concerning his estate as evidenced by the expressions used in his will. It is not very difficult to visualize an unexperienced individual who undertakes the drafting of his will to create various conditions that may appear perfectly clear in his own mind but totally lacking in continuity of thought for someone who has to rely altogether on the expressions for justifying a definite conclusion.

The difficulty of interpretation is whether the testator had in mind exactly the transfers and conditions expressed. Should the court take the position that the terms used were intended to reveal the underlying motive for preparing the will, little confusion would result; but whenever the court considers the expressions used as representing a particular devise or bequest, a strict interpretation of the provisions of the will, no doubt, will become more technical and involved.

Notices to Interested Parties

Before the will is allowed for probation, notices must be sent to all parties having vested interests in the estate, as well as to those who qualify under the statutory provisions of descent and distribution in the absence of the testator's will or in the event the will does not merit probation. Such parties are entitled to this consideration in order that they may have an opportunity to register their objections to the probation of the will provided they are able to present good and justifiable reasons for doing so. It is apparent that the purpose for contesting the probation of the will is to deprive the legatees and devisees from taking under the will, resulting in the estate having to be divided on the statutory basis.

Reliance on Content of Will

The courts are guided by what was contained in the will, and this tends to rule out the possibility of introducing the "parol evidence rule" for showing what was intended by the testator. In the event the introduction of the parol evidence were admissible, the court would be faced with a complicated problem of determining just what could justifiably be relied on and would, without doubt, give encouragement to acts of fraud, duress, undue influence, and perjury while endeavoring to establish the testator's intention.

At the time of filing the will with the Probate Court for probation, the party making the presentment implies that the will is valid and conforms with all statutory requirements for probation. Rather than relying altogether on the completeness and the regularity of the instrument, the court will insist on personal evidence of confirmation. In the absence of any adverse communications claiming certain irregularities of the will, the court must proceed to determine if the will possesses the necessary quality for probation.

It is the privilege of a testator to place the estate and inheritance tax burdens in any manner he desires. In many instances, he will specify the residue out of which such payments are to be made, particularly if such a fund is expected to be sufficiently large. The court was guided by a state statute which protected charitable institutions from having to pay state inheritance taxes, in the absence of any provision in the testator's will to the contrary.[1]

Testator's Intention

The Probate Court assumes the position of endeavoring to clarify certain inconsistencies and irregularities discovered in the testator's will. Had the will been drawn up by an attorney, the court most likely would be more inclined to give a stricter construction to its provisions.

A child of the testator, for example, might claim he or she was unintentionally omitted from the parent's will and for that reason was entitled to share in the estate according to the dis-

[1] Wilson v. Livingston, 507 P 2d 902 (1973).

tribution by law. The issue becomes one of fact to be properly decided by a jury; while if the controversy is one of law, the proper procedure involves a decision to be made by the court.

Expense of Probation

The expense incurred in paying commissions to executors and attorney fees are usually included in the statutory allowances in effect at the time of the decedent's death. Fees will have to be allowed for the witnesses who appear for giving testimony for establishing the genuineness of signatures of the attesting witnesses and also the signing by the testator. The cost of probation will be greatly enhanced when interested parties question the merits of the will for probation in petitioning the court for its contest.

When property belonging to the testator is in the form of real or tangible personal property located in another state, the expense of probation becomes more involved. The executor will either have to qualify as an executor in the foreign state or else arrange for an ancillary administrator in the particular state in which the property is located.

Mislaid or Destroyed Will

Courts are not in agreement relative to the type of evidence necessary for accurately establishing the content of a will which has been mislaid or destroyed subsequent to the testator's death. Some courts apply a very strict rule in maintaining that the provisions claimed for the will must be proven beyond a reasonable doubt. Other courts are less demanding in requiring the evidence submitted to be clear and convincing.

The burden of proof that there had been a duly executed will falls on the party who is petitioning the court for probate proceedings. The court naturally will assume a defensive attitude in requiring the evidence submitted to be either beyond a reasonable doubt or else represent clear and convincing facts as to the essentials of the will including: the date, attesting witnesses, content of the will, and the reason for its loss or destruction.

Prior to the court's accepting any secondary evidence for establishing the validity of a will and reason for its disappearance, the court must be convinced that the facts submitted are true as stated. Assurance must be given to the court that the interested parties have acted with vigilance in making a careful search for the instrument in such places where the deceased normally would be expected to keep important documents for reasons of safety.

When the court is faced with the problem of whether to allow a will to be probated with only secondary evidence to support its validity, it becomes necessary to proceed with great caution. The pertinent information, of course, will include the testimonies of witnesses concerning the lost or destroyed will. To qualify for giving authentic data which will aid and assist the court in arriving at a proper decision, the witnesses must be able to convince the court of their having witnessed the signing by the testator and also the attesting witnesses.

Quality of Will for Probation

Following the death of the testator, the one in possession of the will should petition the proper court within the statutory period for having it probated. Most executors are not familiar with the legal procedure involved, and their discernible shortcomings justify their employing attorneys for performing the legal tasks and for advising the executors in matters pertaining to their duties and responsibilities. The more familiar the executor is with the legal process, the less difficulty will be experienced in getting the will probated and the estate settled. The state in which the real estate is located has jurisdiction over it. Hence, the proper procedure is to file a certified copy of the will, as well as copies of proceedings, with the Probate Court in the county in which such property is located.

The Probate Court has jurisdiction for determining if the will possesses the necessary quality for allowing it to be probated. The affirmative assurance of the court can be established only by the testimonies of attesting witnesses regarding the genuineness of the testator's signature and that it was not obtained under fraud, duress, or undue influence. Assurance is further evidenced by an acquiescence of the beneficiaries and the next of kin who had not expressed any interest toward contesting the probation of the will.

Even though the testator took his own life, this would not constitute conclusive evidence per se that he was insane at the time of drafting his will. This presumption might be raised particularly when there existed only a brief period of time between the drafting of one's will and the taking of his own life. Of course, such an occurrence would tend to establish only circumstantial evidence of a testator's mental incompetency to draft a will; but this would not necessarily represent conclusive evidence.

When someone with considerable wealth is murdered, investigators while searching for motives of the death will certainly not overlook the probability of the act as having been committed by an expected heir. In the absence of any statute denying the right of a beneficiary who had been found responsible for taking the life of the testator, the courts have been consistent in refusing such beneficiary the right of sharing in the estate of the deceased on the theory that to permit the murderer to acquire the amount of the estate to which he would be entitled under normal circumstances would establish a very dangerous precedent and naturally would not be in keeping with accepted public policy.

Should the executor endeavor to have the will probated without the aid of legal counsel, a very embarrassing situation can be created for the court as well as the executor himself. Of course, the court has no duty or responsibility to offer counsel and advice to executors who have failed to engage an attorney to supervise and aid with the legal proceedings.

Power to Revoke

When the discretionary authority of the testator to revoke his will is exercised, the relationship of interested parties, as a result of closeness of kin, is restored to that which prevailed prior to the drafting of the will. In the exercise of his recognized power and right, the testator must have had the mental capacity at the time. Also, the act must have been the result of his intention and free of any influence being unduly exercised over him.

When there exists both a will and a codicil, a question arises as to whether it is possible to revoke one without the other also becoming revoked. In view of the codicil having been written, following the drafting of the will, the revoking of the codicil would in no way affect the provisions of the will.

The beneficiary is privileged to discriminate in determining not to accept certain legacies or devises left him. Rather, in case the gifts are divisible, he can take some and refuse others.

In the event the different types of property intended for the beneficiary are not capable of being separated, the devisee or legatee must accept all of such property or none of it.

When a petition is filed for a protest of a will, the court must decide whether the facts offered to support the probation request are sufficient and adequate for influencing the court to act favorably. Even after a will has been probated, another will bearing a more recent date may be filed with the Probate Court for probation. The court will be responsible for giving consideration to the will bearing the later date. In doing so, the court will raise the question as to why the later will had been withheld longer than the statutory period before offering it for probation.

Interested parties in a will can always question its probation quality, and it is left to the discretion of the Probate Court to determine whether the reasons are justifiable for the court to act in denying further probation procedure. Meanwhile, the court is obligated, in the interest of promoting justice, to carefully examine the evidence submitted by parties having an interest in the estate, which is adverse to the provisions in the will, before making the final decision as to the disposition to be made of the will.

Priorities in Settling Claims

Priorities, of course, may be regulated by statute; but ordinarily the following pattern represents the first in order of time for settling claims against the estate:

(a) The funeral expenses of the deceased are recognized as being necessary and must be given first consideration.

(b) In classifying creditors as to preference in the payment of debts, first of all will be the preferred creditors, including federal and state governments in this order.

(c) Judgments which previously had been allowed by the courts.

(d) Debts of the deceased secured by a mortgage lien.

(e) Wages due employees.

(f) Payment of unsecured claims against the estate.

After satisfying the claims of creditors having priorities, the statute of the state in which the will is being probated must be observed.

Chapter 13

Deficiencies of Wills

Conceding that a testator possesses adequate mental faculties for indicating in his last will and testament the beneficiaries to whom his property will go at his death, statutes have been enacted in the various states for protecting the interests of heirs who otherwise would have vested claims against the estate had the deceased died intestate or the will should be declared invalid for probation.

Circumstances at times make it possible for certain parties, often representing next of kin, who were able to spend much time with the testator just prior to his death to take advantage of the favorable position for exercising an undue amount of influence over him in the drafting of his will. It is not to be presumed that some influence cannot rightly be exercised over the testator, but the court must decide whether such influence was excessive and undue as to justify the Probate Court in refusing to allow the will to be probated.

Failure to Identify Parties

A probation problem is presented when an attesting witness to a will is dead at the time the will is offered for probation. Some states require only two witnesses, while other states require three in number. The testator at the time of drafting the will might wish to allow for a possible unforeseen difficulty of one of the witnesses being disqualified by way of naming more than the minimum number required by law so as to provide a successful safeguard in the event one of the witnesses should be prohibited from serving. When it becomes obvious that a witness could not give testimony due to poor health, or perhaps it would be inconvenient for him to appear in court due to his having moved a long distance away, or since the execution of the will, a witness had died, the testator, in such instances, would be acting wisely in drafting a new will even though the court, no doubt, would be guided by the capacity of the witnesses at the time of the execution of the will.

Whenever a testator dies a number of years following the drafting of his will, the discretion of the court may be exercised in not requiring the attesting witnesses to appear and give testimony even though they might be living at the time. In such instances, anyone wishing to contest a will executed a number of years ago would have little chance of establishing sound reasons for challenging the capacity of the testator, the qualification of the attesting witnesses, the intention of the testator, a mistake in the drafting of the will, or that fraud, duress, or undue influence had been exercised which would tend to establish the invalidity of the will.

When the testator employs a draftsman, all of the facts will be given concerning his intention as to definite transfers of real and personal property which will become effective at the testator's death. When a mistake is made by the draftsman and is not detected until later, courts will allow corrections in the identity of parties when it is unmistakably clear that certain provisions in the testator's will did not express the intention of the testator.

Draftsman's Error

The testator, in an Ohio[1] decision, instructed the draftsman to prepare for him a will in which a particular grandnephew was to be declared the residuary legatee. The will was signed by the testator believing that such provision was included. The question was raised as to whether the will should be allowed for probation in view of the mistake. The court concluded that the will was entitled to probation despite the failure of the draftsman to carry out the instructions of the testator. The court was convinced that a mistake had been made by the draftsman.

A mistake by the draftsman in a Maryland[2] case concerned the residuary clause. At the time of the execution of the will,

1 Johnson v. Ramsey, 18 Ohio App 321, 90 ALR 2d 945 (1923).

2 Lyon v. Townsend, 124 Md 163, 91 A 704, 90 ALR (2d) 936 (1914).

the testatrix was in the anesthesia room of a hospital prior to an operation which proved to be fatal to her. Drugs had been administered to her just before the will was handed to her for her to read and to sign. While reading the will, she temporarily lost consciousness. The court reasoned that it would be a strange situation if the testatrix could read the will with full knowledge of its content under the circumstances, and ruled that the testatrix could not be held responsible for the mistake of the draftsman.

Where a testator devised a life estate in his realty to his widow and the remainder vesting in his children, a provision was made that should a child die "intestate" prior to the probation of the will or before the death of his widow, the estate should be divided among those children living. The scrivener, in drafting the will, substituted the term "without issue" for the expression "intestate," believing that the terms were synonymous in meaning. Nevertheless, the court contended that the meaning was clear, and there was no occasion for confusing the meaning of an expression which was definite in construction. The court concluded that no reason could be offered for determining the meaning of the testatrix other than that which had been clearly stated.

Codicil Reveals Changes

In case a will is altered prior to its execution, those who would be affected adversely as a result of the changes would naturally look with suspicion on the discrepancies. The testator can avoid future controversies concerning the content and the quality of the will in making the provisions definite, crystal clear, and at the same time containing no indication of suspicion of any irregularities. When an alteration is made after the execution of the will, either the entire will or certain parts of it might be declared invalid. The will itself would not be affected by an alteration of the codicil.

A testatrix in Alabama[3] had drafted a will in the year 1939 and another in 1941, which, according to the law of wills, revoked the earlier will. A codicil was prepared in 1947, but it was not clear as to whether the codicil became a part of the 1941 or the 1939 will. The two wills were practically identical,

[3] Fuller v. Nazal, 259 Ala 598, 67 S 2d 806, 90 ALR 2d 947 (1953).

with minor changes. The scrivener of the codicil referred to the formalities in the testator's 1939 will, including the date, last will and testament, and signatures of the testator and the witnesses. The testatrix's banker, and also the attorney who drafted the codicil, contended that the reference in the codicil to the 1939 will was a mistake of the draftsman and that the testatrix had not intended to revoke the 1941 will. The trial court agreed that the codicil was intended to apply to the 1941 will, to which the reviewing court agreed.

Naming of Beneficiaries

A testatrix, whose domicile was in New York,[4] engaged a draftsman to prepare for her a will leaving all of her estate to her children to share equally. The name of one of the children was omitted in the testamentary trust created for her children. After the will was drafted, the evidence showed that its content was read to the testatrix. The court admitted the will to be probated even though there was an omission of one of her children.

In the state of Iowa,[5] a testator instructed his attorney to draft his will and to prepare it in such a manner as to prevent the husband of his daughter from subsequently getting any of his estate. The attorney did not know that the daughter and her husband were divorced. Rather, he was of the opinion that they were merely separated. A testamentary trust was provided in the will for the daughter's life estate and naming her children as remaindermen. Such provision might have eventually resulted in the husband's realizing a future claim against the estate should his former wife and one or more of his children predecease him.

At the time of the drafting of the will, the attorney did not have knowledge of the daughter's divorce; but at the time the will was read to the testator, the attorney knew of the divorce. Due to the weakened condition of the testator, the attorney decided the will should be executed as drafted. The court contended that the mistake was material. The testator was near death when he signed the will, and the attorney's knowledge of the facts before the will was executed made the will invalid.

[4] Re Forbes' Will, 14 NYS 460, 90 ALR 2d 945 (1891).

[5] Re Kempthorne's Estate, 188 Iowa 70, 175 NW 857, 90 ALR (2d) 943 (1920).

An attorney was engaged by a testator in the state of Vermont[6] to draft for him a will. The instructions were that the testator's brother was to be omitted from receiving any benefits from his estate. The will, as drawn, left everything to a friend with a provision that should the beneficiary predecease the testator, the estate would be distributed in accordance with the law of descent and distribution. While the draft of the will differed from the exact wish of the testator, the court concluded that since there was not present any undue influence and the will had been read to the testator, nothing could be done to prevent the brother from being included among the bodily heirs of the deceased.

Partial Irregularities

Some courts observe the principle of strict interpretation of a will in contending that if some part of the will does not qualify for probation, the entire will is void. The fact cannot be overlooked that parts of the will are capable of being regular and valid. In taking the position that a will must be valid by wholes and not by parts, courts may be said to be following the line of least resistance. However, modern decisions favor the rule that a will can be valid in some parts and invalid in other parts while qualifying for probation as to the portion of the will which is regular.

The Probate Court has the responsibility of determining whether certain parts of a will should be declared unenforceable because of the exercise of undue influence over the testator by an interested party. To what extent is such influence to be considered reasonable and permissible is for the court to determine. Certainly, not all influence, irregardless of how slight it might be, could move the court to act negatively in passing on the legal merits of the will.

Should there be a mistake with respect to the identity of the instrument itself, the petition for having the entire will set aside would have justification. The nature of the mistake might relate to the testator's not having an understanding as to the actual content of the will, or else he might have been influenced into signing his last will and testament without any awareness regarding the actual content of the instrument. Too many indi-

---

[6] Estate of Burt, 122 Vt 260, 169 A 2d 32, 90 ALR 2d 941 (1961).

viduals will be inclined to take things on faith after having employed some well-informed person to draft a will and then sign any instrument which is presented to them for their signatures. The witnesses, moreover, can be of no assistance in the interpretation of the content of the will.

Incompetent Attestation

The Probate Court will be most concerned with the evidence establishing competency of witnesses at the time of the execution of the will and not necessarily at the time of probation. The testimony of a witness who was mentally alert at the time of probation of the will would have greater influence with the court than one having a mental deficiency at the time of probation. This being true, the testator would be acting wisely upon discovering the mental incapacity of a witness to his will to draft another will and have other parties sign as attesting witnesses. Another precaution would be to have more witnesses than the law required so that if one witness should be declared incompetent to testify, the other competent witnesses would satisfy the legal requirement.

It becomes a very unfortunate situation for beneficiaries of a will, when the court declares it to be invalid because of failure of the testator to strictly comply with the law, in neglecting to have at least the number of competent witnesses which the law prescribes. In the states which recognize the holographic will (written in the testator's own handwriting), the statute may or may not require attestation. In view of the technicalities of the law which prescribes definite standards for probation, it is not advisable to follow the line of least resistance in omitting the attestation part of one's will when it is feasible to have it properly witnessed.

Results of Undue Influence

Being able to draw a definite line between what constitutes reasonable influence exercised over a testator in causing him to prepare a will and an undue amount of influence does indeed on occasions present a real question of controversy. The court would have to decide the extent of influence which would result in the testator's being denied the privilege of acting as a free agent. To this end, the question might be raised as to what would likely have been the decision had the testator not acted under a great amount of pressure.

The court will not be inclined to look with disfavor on the influence exercised by husband or wife over each other in the execution of a will. Their positions differ from all others, because if one spouse is dissatisfied with the will of the other at the time of probation, the survivor has the option of taking either by law or under the will. The influence exercised by others (particularly the children) in courting favors of the testator will receive a close look by the court in determining the justification of the testator's favoring one child over the others.

When one desires to execute a will while in his declining years or during his last illness, the court will look for indications of undue influence which has been exercised particularly when dissatisfaction is expressed by various ones possessing vested interests in the estate. The petitions to contest a will which has been filed with the Probate Court will request the court to declare the will invalid and instead designate the estate to be divided among the heirs at law.

Protection of Heirs

Possessed with a low mentality while exercising ownership in a considerable amount of property tends to make one a target for the exercise of undue influence over such an individual, insofar as his testamentary gifts might seem to indicate. Selfish motives, especially on the part of close relatives, are often the basis of their taking advantage of the testator's mental weakness in influencing his decisions in the bequests and devises in his will. The court owes a duty to give such an incompetent person the full protection of the law.

It is not for the court to dictate to the testator the exact manner in which his will should be drawn. Making testamentary commitments is a personal matter and a high privilege of the testator. The important concern of the court is that someone will not take advantage of the weaknesses of the testator for one's own self-enrichment. Should a testator endeavor to leave his spouse or children out of his will and give everything to a charitable or religious organization, or to a distant relative, or a friend, the court would consider the unfairness of such dispositions and would naturally inquire into the motives behind the testator's devises and bequests.

Detecting Fraud in the Inducement

In order to constitute fraud, the statements must not only be false, but they must he made with knowledge of their falsities. They must have been made with the motive in mind to get the particular party to act on them; and such a party acted accordingly while justifiably relying on the truthfulness of the misleading statements, resulting in the suffering of a loss. The term fraud as applied to a will is a cunning or a deceitful practice by which the testator is misled in the disposing of his property because of the testator's possessing convictions that the false statements were true. Fraud might result from withholding from the testator pertinent data equivalent to unduly influencing the testator in the disposition of his property.

In very unusual situations, following the probation of a will, evidence of fraud have been discovered which unquestionably unduly influenced the testator in disposing of his property in a manner which he likely would not have done had he possessed knowledge of the true facts. In such cases, courts have recognized petitions for rescinding the probation procedure and declaring the will void, thus leaving the estate to be divided in accordance with the statutory provisions.

Chapter 14

Obligations of the Estate

Anyone possessing an interest in the estate of the deceased may protect such right by means of registering his protest with the Probate Court and calling attention to certain deficiencies in the will of the deceased at the time of its execution as justifiable reasons for having the will declared invalid and not meriting probation quality. In the event the probation of the will is denied, the liquidation of the estate, according to the statutory regulations of descent and distribution, will resemble closely the following outline of procedure:

(a) Surviving spouse to receive the first consideration.
(b) Children of the deceased or their lineal descendants.
(c) Parents of the deceased.
(d) Brothers and sisters of the deceased or their descendants.
(e) Paternal and maternal grandparents or their descendants.
(f) Next of kin.
(g) Stepchildren or their lineal descendants.
(h) Escheat to the state.

Claims of Widow

The facts in a Kentucky[1] decision concerned a husband who left a will in which his widow was left exactly the portion of his estate to which she would have been entitled had she decided to take under the intestate law. The widow claimed tes-

[1] Murphy v. Murphy, 23 Ky 1460, 65 SW 165, 78 ALR 2d 1065 (1901).

tamentary incapacity and undue influence exercised over her husband in his last will; while in his previous will, she had been given a life interest in his entire state. The court would not allow a contest of the will, because she would take the same amount under the will as the law would allow. As to the previous will in which she was left a life estate in all of his property, the court would not allow the evidence to be introduced, since such a will was not in existence and could have been revoked many years ago, stated the court.

The above-mentioned decision is inconsistent with the reasoning of other courts on this subject. In a Nebraska[2] case, a husband in his will left his widow what was equivalent to the amount she could expect by law. This did not rule out her right of protest. The court maintained that when a will is deposited with the Probate Court, along with a petition for probation, the duty of the court is to set aside a definite time and place during which all interested parties may register their objections to the probation of the will. This included not only the named beneficiaries, but also many other interested parties.

A Missouri[3] court was very definite in ruling that in most circumstances, a widow could not contest the will of her deceased husband who had left her one-half of the real and personal property which was identical to the amount to which she would be entitled under the law of descent and distribution.

It is generally recognized that a widow has the right to contest the will of her deceased husband when she is capable of showing that his will was the result of undue influence having been exercised over him by the executor or other interested parties. The cause to be cited in such an instance would likely be the incapacity of her husband to bequeath and devise his estate.

Drafting Discrepancies

It was ruled in an Indiana[4] decision that a will cannot be contested merely on the theory that the draftsman was in error as to the manner in which the property was to be disposed of.

---

[2] Re Drake's Estate, 150 Neb 568, 35 NW 2d 417, 78 ALR 2d 1064 (1948).

[3] Jensen v. Hendricks, 338 Mo 459, 92 SW 2d 108, 78 ALR 2d 1064 (1936).

[4] Rapp v. Reehling, 124 Ind 36, 23 NE 777 (1890).

This rule has also applied in other situations where the testator had language difficulty. In either case, when the will was read and explained to the testator prior to the execution of his will, he thereby becomes compelled to assume the responsibility of error committed by the draftsman.

A protest was offered in New Jersey[5] to the probation of a will on the ground that the testator did not understand the provisions which the draftsman had inserted in the will which was read to the testator prior to his signing it. The testator kept the will in his possession for three and one-half years until he wished to have a codicil attached to his last will and testament. Such provisions in the codicil ratified all of the clauses in his original will except the matter of taking a small amount from the residue and applying it toward a special bequest. The court reasoned that the slight change in the testator's will by means of a codicil did not make the will invalid.

Protests were offered to the probation of a will in Wisconsin[6] on the principle of inadequate mental capacity of the testator. The will mentioned that the residuary would go to the testator's nieces and nephews living in Norway. Actually, the testator had only nephews and no nieces living in the foreign country. The lawyer confessed his error in inserting the word "nieces" when the testator had no such nieces. In reviewing the trial court's decision of recognizing the will for its probation quality, the court contended that the term "nieces" could be considered only as surplusage and of no particular legal significance.

Descent and Distribution

When the Probate Court is petitioned by a dissatisfied party who claims to have a vested interest in the estate of the deceased, it becomes obvious that such a motive expressed is purely a selfish one. He entertains the hope of realizing more should the will be set aside and denied its probation, thereby making necessary the dividing of the estate according to the law of descent and distribution. Only when a will fails to satisfy all legal requirements for probation will the court allow the estate of the deceased to be divided among the legal heirs.

[5] Re Triebe's Will, 114 NJ 227, 168 A 404, 90 ALR 2d 945 (1933).

[6] Klagstad's Will, 264 Wis 269, 58 NW 2d 636, 90 ALR 2d 946 (1953).

In the state of Massachusetts,[7] a husband who had been convicted and sentenced to the penitentiary for life raised the question as to whether or not he was entitled to the right under the law of contesting the will of his deceased wife whose place of domicile was New York state. Since the New York statute described a person convicted for life as being civilly dead, a husband serving a life sentence in Massachusetts could not contest the will of his deceased wife who resided in New York.

Right of Vested Interests

Generally, those who are instrumental in establishing a cause for contesting a will are closely related to the testator and would likely receive a larger share of the estate of the deceased, in the absence of a will. Had one been omitted altogether in the testator's will, his right of attacking the validity of the will would appear more definite and certain.

When an interested party in the estate registers his disapproval to the probation of the will, the court will appoint a time during which testimonies can be given favoring the probation of the will, as well as the offering of objections to its enforcement. In attacking the will, those having adverse interests to the probation of the instrument will raise various questions concerning the capacity of the testator, qualifications of the witnesses, the effect of changes in the marital status of the deceased, the nature of the property devised or bequeathed, the revocation of the will, or the defects of the will due to mistakes or the exercise of fraud, duress, or undue influence over the testator in the execution of his will.

The age of the testator of a will, under certain conditions, might influence the court to contend that the execution of the will was a result of undue influence. At the age of 91 years, a woman, through the assistance of others who helped to steady her, signed her name to her will. The fact that such assistance was given her, coupled with the failure of interested parties to read her will to her, or to have the testator sign or initial each page of the will, were cited for justifying the protest to the probation of the will. In view of the fact that the evidence showed that the testatrix had not been coerced into the signing of her will, the court allowed it to be probated.[8]

[7] Re Lindewall's Will, 287 NY 347, 39 NE 2d 907, 139 ALR 1301 (1942).

[8] Re Barouquet's Will, 148 So 2d 836, 98 ALR 2d 820 (1963).

Courts are not in sympathy with the "no contest" clause mentioned in some wills. The expression endeavors to protect the will from any protest procedure exercised by interested parties. It provides that if any beneficiary attempts to contest the will, his rights to any of the estate will be curtailed. Such an attitude on the part of the testator would indicate that he had obvious convictions as to the manner in which his property was to be divided, and was strongly opposed to an attempt of any interested party to have his proposed plan of distribution of his estate changed or altered in any form.

As a rule, a will is probated in its entirety. However, certain provisions in a will might be contested due to mistakes as to the identity of the parties or subject matter. At the same time, the will may not be attacked in its entirety. Prior to the court's allowing a will for probate, certain information will have to be provided regarding the testator or beneficiaries which might justify the court's declaring at least portions of the will to be invalid.

Particularly when a will is quite detailed and involved, it is possible that the court will allow parts of the will to be deleted from the will because of illegality. Under those circumstances, there would be little justification for declaring the entire will to be invalid, resulting in considerable confusion and dissatisfaction on the part of beneficiaries, in view of all of the other parts being recognized as legal.

Protests Subsequent to Probate

The general rule as applied to the probation of wills is that once the legatee or devisee has acquired the benefits under the will, he cannot later proceed to contest its validity. Other courts take the position that whenever a beneficiary in good faith receives benefits under a will, he would be prohibited from receiving additional benefits. Conditions, of course, can bring about changes and exceptions. Thus, the modern weight of authority is that whenever a beneficiary receives benefits according to the will without any knowledge of his additional rights or any deficiencies in the will of the testator, such as fraud, duress, or undue influence which had been exercised over the testator, the innocent beneficiary will be given an opportunity to question the validity of the testator's will even though probation procedures had been executed. Courts have held that even though the will had been probated, the beneficiary, nevertheless, had a right to surrender his share of the estate and to register his protest to the will.

Time of Probation

In offering objections by parties having a vested interest in the estate to the probation of the will, a petition must be filed with the Probate Court within a reasonable time, which is usually prescribed by the statutory regulation. The court would not be inclined to interpret the law strictly against beneficiaries who are absent temporarily from their places of domicile, living in a foreign country, or suffering from a mental or physical ailment.

The state of Ohio, for example, allows interested parties six months, following the time of presentment for probation, to offer a contest to the probation procedure. Exceptions are also made in the case of a beneficiary suffering from a legal disability to be allowed six months from the time the disability is removed.

Justifiable Causes for Contests

Few cases have reached the courts concerning the legality of a will which attempts to discourage the advancement of religion, particularly the Christian faith, while encouraging the spread of atheism. Courts have been cautious in denying the privilege to testators to minimize the existence of a supernatural power by way of making devises and bequests of property to certain organizations which are known to be opposed to the promotion of Christian principles and ideals.

Interested parties desiring to offer a protest to the will filed for probation are required to submit to the Probate Court justifiable reasons for doing so:

(a) Incompetency of the testator, including tenderness of age, mental or physical incapacity, or advanced age.

(b) Incompetency of witnesses, either an insufficient number or one's failure to qualify.

(c) Testator persuaded by fraud, duress, or undue influence.

(d) Destruction of the will or its revocation by a new one.

(e) Material alteration subsequent to the execution of the will.

(f) Failure to offer the will for probation within the statutory period.
(g) Inconsistencies and lack of clearness.
(h) Failure to include surviving spouse.
(i) Omission of names of bodily heirs.

Chapter 15

Executor's Rights and Responsibilities

An executor's authority is regulated by the terms of the will, as well as the statutory law of the particular state. His main concern, naturally, is that of liquidating the estate as quickly as possible and to properly prorate the proceeds. This endeavor might take only a relatively short period of time, or the procedure could possibly extend over one or more years, depending on a number of factors, including: (1) size of the estate; (2) nature of the property; (3) number of creditors; or (4) situs of the property.

In case a business, farm, or other real property is included in the estate, the will might very well give the executor discretionary authority to operate the business or farm and to rent the realty until, in his judgment, the time becomes most opportune for disposing of it for the highest possible consideration. In view of this possibility of broad power having been given the executor, the time needed for winding up the estate could be longer than that which many of the beneficiaries would likely consider to be reasonable.

Liquidating the Estate

While carrying out the directives of the testator, the executor will be expected to exercise reasonable diligence in liquidating the estate, but not at the expense of realizing returns too small due to the time for disposing of the property being quite unsatisfactory. Parties having vested interests in the estate may appear overly anxious for acquiring their shares as quickly as possible, and thus become quite critical of the executor's endeavor to exercise reasonable diligence in his fiduciary capacity.

The executor more or less takes over the management of the affairs of the deceased even by way of aiding in the planning of the funeral. In the absence of his familiarity with the legal procedure, he has the privilege of engaging an attorney to perform the legal tasks. On occasions, an attorney is nominated by the deceased to serve as executor of the estate. Such an appointment has its advantages in that speedier action can be assured due to the attorney's knowledge of the legal aspects of the principles involving wills. It is also a common practice for the attorney who drafted the will to be named the executor.

After the nomination of the executor has received the confirmation of the court, the first task (usually with the aid of an attorney) is to petition the Probate Court for the appropriation of a portion of the estate (ordinarily a year's allowance) for the surviving spouse and the children while the will is in the process of being probated. Some state statutes make special provisions for such emergencies.

Prior to the proceeding to liquidate the estate, the executor must, first of all, prepare a statement as to the debts due the estate, as well as the obligations of the estate. Claims will be filed for debts due the firm, consisting of insurance proceeds, dividends, interests, past-due promissory notes due the estate, rents, and open book accounts which should have been paid previously. Current obligations of the estate which should receive the immediate attention of the executor might be in the form of insurance premiums on property of the estate, mortgage payments, notes payable, rent payable, and taxes, including federal, state, and local. If the rights and obligations of the estate are indefinite and confusing, the executor has the right to enter into a compromise arrangement. Converting certain property of the estate into cash could be a very slow and difficult process. Circumstances might dictate to the executor whether it would be advisable in some instances to conduct either a public or a private sale.

In a recent New York[1] court decision, it was disclosed that the residue, out of which the debts, cost of administration, and taxes were to be paid, was inadequate for meeting such obligations of the deceased. The controversy concerned whether the

[1] Kramer v. Surrogate Court of N.Y. County, 356 N.Y. Supp 2d 984 (1974).

residuary or specific legatees should be expected to supplement the residue in the settling of the estate. The court reasoned that the residuary legatees were responsible for meeting the deficiency.

Control Over Growing Crops

In the absence of any provision in the testator's will indicating to whom growing crops are to go, the court has the responsibility of determining the classification of the property, according to real or personal, before making a final decision as to the right of ownership. In the case of a deceased who dies intestate, the real property goes directly to the heirs at law, while the personal property will go to the legal representative, the executor or administrator.

A New York[2] court ruled that the proceeds from the sale of hay, which was growing at the time of the owner's death, belonged to the life tenant, since growing grass was a part of the realty and should descend to the heir or devisee. The law distinguishes between growing crops, which come about as a result of cultivation by man, and the so-called natural crops which grow spontaneously, such as hay, according to the reasoning of the court.

The following court citations emphasize quite clearly the widespread agreement of courts in the various states that growing crops represent personal property and rightly go to the legal representative of the deceased:

(a) At the time of the testator's death in Kansas,[3] there was growing wheat which had not as yet been harvested. The court contended that the growing crop at the time of the testator's death belonged to the executor or the administrator and not to the divisee of the land.

(b) Cotton was growing in Mississippi on the testator's plantation at the time of his death. The court ruled that it must pass to the testator's personal representative who was responsible for applying it toward the settling of the estate and in paying the debts of the deceased.

(c) At the testator's death, he had a crop in the cultivation process. The court declared the growing crop to be personal property, to which the administrator was entitled to apply toward the payment of debts of the deceased, and thus did not go to the heirs at law.[4]

---

[2] Re Chamberlain's Estate, 140 NY 390, 35 NE 602, 92 ALR 2d

[3] Kesler v. Heberling, 13 Kan 571, 213 P 639, 92 ALR 2d 1383

[4] Re Kupp's Estate, 92 ALR 2d 138 (1868).

(d) To avoid confusion, the testator had the privilege of setting forth in his will the exact party to whom the growing crops at the time of his death should go. A North Carolina[5] case reports a clear intention expressed by the testator in the execution of his will providing for the growing crops to pass separately from the land and not to be considered as going with the legal ownership of the land. Hence, the executor was given the discretion of renting the land, which, of course, implied that the executor was entitled to the crops.

(e) As recorded in a Virginia[6] will, there was a devise of land which included growing crops and crops which had been harvested. There was no question as to the right of the devisee not only to the crops growing, but also those which had been carried over from the preceding year and also crops brought in from the adjoining plantations.

(f) A Missouri[7] case records a testator's will which specifically provided for perishable property, such as mules, horses, harvested crops, and other personal property to go to the executor for the purpose of converting them into cash. The court reasoned that personal property listed as perishables did not go with the land which was devised to the plaintiff.

(g) An Illinois[8] statute held that growing crops should pass to the legal representative. Thus, the court recognized the right of the executor to sell the growing crops of the intestate at the time of his death and to use the proceeds for paying the debts of the deceased. Instead of the growing crops going to the two sons of the testator, they went to the administrator in accordance with the statute.

Qualifications of Executor

In some instances, members of a particular family have for a number of years considered a certain attorney as their legal counsellor and representative in all legal matters. In considering the qualifications of an executor, the testator is expected to give a great deal of emphasis to the fiduciary's possessing adequate legal knowledge, since a will involves a considerable amount of legal environment. Thus, an attorney is placed in a favorable position for serving successfully in a twofold capacity,

---

[5] Tayler v. Bond, 45 NC 5, 92 ALR 2d 1380 (1852).

[6] Carnagy v. Woodcock, 16 Va 234, 92 ALR 2d 1380 (1811).

[7] Pratte v. Coffman, Executor, 27 Mo 424, 92 ALR 2d 1381 (1858).

[8] Choney v. Roadhouse, 32 Ill App 49, 92 ALR 2d 1383 (1889).

such as executing the legal matters in addition to his acting as the testator's legal representative in liquidating the estate for which he would be justified in collecting for both services.

A testator who is operating a farm or a business at the time of his death might very well place his heirs or legal representative in quite an embarrassing position should he die quite suddenly without carefully planning a definite procedure for making the transition of ownership. If it is intended that the executor is to be given a wide discretion in the operation of the farm or business or to lease the real property, a full and clear disclosure of the arrangement should be made unmistakably clear to the executor and to the heirs as well.

Executor Versus Trustee Capacities

Even if it is not expressed in the testator's will, the executor owes a duty to protect the estate of the deceased before there is a legal confirmation of his appointment by the Probate Court. This will involve his assisting in the burial arrangements and serving in a supervisory capacity until he receives from the court his letter of testamentary, or his letter of administration should he be appointed by the court, which is evidence of his authority in assuming control over the estate. The personal property will be used for paying the debts and funeral expenses of the deceased; and if such amount proves to be inadequate, the executor has the right to levy against as much of the real property as is necessary.

The executor has the responsibility of closing out the estate within a reasonable time, while the trustee will take title to the property under the will of the testator; but the actual possession thereof must come through the executor or administrator. The trustee will be guided by the terms in the trust arrangement for distributing the income prior to the passing of title to the remainderman after the lapse of a specified time or upon the happening of a designated contingency.

An executor does not take title to the property. Instead, he acts in a fiduciary capacity, and, as such, he owes a duty to act in good faith. His duties will be terminated after the estate has been liquidated and the proceeds have been properly prorated. The trustee, meanwhile, takes title subject to the equitable obligation to maintain control over the property for a definite period of time or until the happening of a stated contingency, at which time the title vests in the remainderman. Frequently, according to the provisions in the testator's will, such fiduciary's responsibility might be twofold; namely, serving both as an executor and a trustee. Incidentally, one's duty as trustee will continue following the discharge of his executor's obligations. When one individual performs in a duo capacity as executor and trustee, the time necessarily required toward administering the estate will, no doubt, be greater for which he is entitled to include charges for services in both capacities.

Duties Exercised by Fiduciaries

In drafting a will, it may be expressed or implied that the effectiveness of the instrument will date from the death of the testator. The functions of the executor necessarily must be in accordance with the wishes of the testator as revealed in his last will. The court, as well as the beneficiaries, can insist that the executor act with proper and reasonable diligence in the liquidating process. Neither can the testator prescribe in his will so-called delaying tactics by way of including certain conditions for transferring the title to particular beneficiaries until some future time or upon the happening of certain contingencies.

The District Court[9] of the state of Utah recognized the right of the executrix to pay inheritance taxes prior to making distributions of the estate. Such taxes were to be classed as estate expense to be shared by all beneficiaries, including the wife, whose share of the residuary was adequate for satisfying her claim of marital deduction.

When the testator is interested in designating in his will a postponement of action, he should create a testamentary trust, indicating that subsequent to his death, the title to certain property would pass to a recommended trustee who would care for the property according to the provisions in the trust arrangement until the title eventually will pass to the remainderman.

Executor's Remuneration

The executor or administrator's right to compensation for services rendered is either expressed in the testator's will or such is to be implied. Unless the executor is a member of the family and personally has a vested interest in the estate, or is a close friend of the family, he will naturally expect adequate remuneration for his services rendered. One advantage in selecting a member of the family to assume the responsibility of exe-

[9] Thayn, Executrix v. United States, 386 F Supp 245 (1974).

cuting the testator's wishes is for economy reasons in reducing the expense of administering the estate. A testator might desire to avoid a discussion with the named executor concerning the problem of procedure at the testator's death. Conversely, much would be gained in time, money, and effort if the testator had endeavored to groom the executor for assuming his fiduciary duties in the future.

Reasonable compensation for the executor or administrator will be determined by the size of the estate, nature of the property, number of beneficiaries, extent of authority assumed, the amount of time devoted to the liquidating of the estate, and the time necessary for winding up the affairs of the estate.

Executor's Discretion

A provision in the English Statute of Frauds, which has been incorporated into the laws of the respective states, for protecting the fiduciary concerns a promise of an executor or administrator to answer for the debts of the deceased out of his own estate must be in writing in order to be enforceable at law. If there were no such protection under the law for the executor, the opportunity for unscrupulous parties to exploit him would be so prominent and tempting until it would become very difficult to find qualified persons to assume this responsibility.

The "parol evidence rule" is not to be confused with the promise of an executor or administrator to compensate an interested party if he will promise not to offer a contest to the testator's will. Such an individual promise does not have to be in writing in order to be enforceable against the executor or administrator.

Prior to the testator's mentioning an executor in his will, he should, first of all, receive the confirmation of the executor as to his willingness to accept the obligation. Even after the giving of an affirmative response, subsequent happenings might influence the executor not to accept the appointment for the following reasons:

(a) The estate being quite small, the compensation would be inadequate.
(b) The task appearing too time-consuming.
(c) Poor health of the executor.
(d) Estate too large and too involved.
(e) Lack of confidence in one's capacity.
(f) Sufficient discretionary authority lacking.
(g) Unsympathetic attitude of beneficiaries.
(h) Beneficiaries too demanding.
(i) Time involved too long and drawn-out.

Part III

Tax Problems and Procedures

Chapter 16

Reasons for Property Transfers

The estate of a deceased, which might be subject to the federal estate or state succession taxes, will include not only property passing under a will, but also that which the testator had transferred during his lifetime in contemplation of death. As one approaches old age, he naturally considers the years ahead as representing the possibility of his living. He might conclude, also, that his life expectancy could not be longer than a few years at the most, after which all of his right of ownership to his entire estate would have to be entrusted to others.

One alternative for an individual's planning his estate is to make outright gifts while living. In case he desires to maintain control over his property during his lifetime, he may draft a will indicating to whom each item of property ownership will go after his death. The third thing he may do is to follow the line of least resistance in not making any plans for the future and have his property divided according to the law of descent and distribution at his death. In determining the amount of tax which should be paid to the state, and possibly the federal government, for the privilege of the testator's naming the transferees and also for the privilege of the beneficiaries in acquiring the estate, the government will consider the motives for the subsequent transferring of ownership of property.

In Anticipation of Dying

In order to determine the amount of tax which should be assessed against the estate of the deceased, the court will be concerned in discovering if the transfers were made in contemplation of death. Thus, a number of factors will be taken into consideration:

(a) Nature of the conveyance.
(b) Time of the transfer.
(c) Age of the transferor.
(d) Transferor's physical and mental condition.
(e) Type of property involved.
(f) Value of the estate.
(g) Number of beneficiaries.
(h) Discrimination as to naming of beneficiaries.
(i) Possibility of undue influence exercised.
(j) Conditional transfers.
(k) Marital status.

After considering the various conditions which could have influenced the testator, the court will conclude as to the underlying reasons for the change of ownership. Even though a testator may make either an outright gift of property or a testamentary provision for a future transfer when he realizes his days are numbered, this might not represent such poor judgment provided he had the capacity to make the transfer and was not unduly influenced by others in doing so. While the transfer would be included in the gross estate for federal estate tax purposes, it would not be subject to the federal gift tax.

Purpose of Gift

The question was raised in an Ohio[1] decision as to whether a gift inter vivos of a parent to his children represented an act of generosity or a gift in contemplation of death. The court reasoned that if such a gift was made for the purpose of relieving the needs of one's children, it would have to be interpreted as an act of generosity; but if the gift during one's lifetime was made by way of equalizing the transfer with previous gifts to other children, then it would have to be considered a transfer in contemplation of death and subject to tax.

The facts revealed that in 1932, the deceased gave 150 shares of stock to her daughter and only 50 shares to her son. In 1935, she gave 100 shares to her son to equalize the former gift to her daughter. The court concluded that the gifts in 1932 were not made in contemplation of death, nor were the trans-

[1] Estate of Robinson, 145 OS 55 (1945).

fers to take effect in possession or enjoyment at or after the death of the donor. As to the gift in 1935 of 100 shares to equalize a former transfer, the court ruled that it must be considered a transfer in contemplation of death and subject to the estate tax.

Section 2012 of the *1954 Internal Revenue Code* clears up the question of adjustments in cases involving double taxation:

> "If a tax on a gift has been paid and thereafter on the death of the donor any amount in respect of such gift is to be included in the value of the gross estate of the decedent, then there should be credited against the tax imposed the amount of the tax paid on a gift with respect to so much of the property which constituted the gift as is included in the gross estate, except that the amount of such credit shall not exceed an amount which bears the same ratio to the tax imposed (after deducting from such tax the credit for state death taxes) as the value (at the time of the gift or at the time of the death, whichever is lower) of so much of the property which constituted the gift as is included in the gross estate bears to the value of the entire gross estate reduced by the aggregrate amount of the charitable and marital deductions allowed."

Health Factor

The court will take into consideration the health conditions of the donor at the time of making the disposition in determining if the transfer was made in contemplation of death. One's illness at the time of making the transfer will merely serve to establish circumstantial evidence but not conclusive evidence as to the reason for his action. The Supreme Court[2] explained that whenever one is stricken with a disease which is fatal, even though immediate death is not expected, such transfers would be in contemplation of death.

Whenever the facts reveal that the donor was suffering with an incurable disease when he made a decision to transfer the ownership of his property, it would present a simple problem for the court in presuming that the transfer was made in contemplation of death. No such conclusion could be drawn, however, had the donor been inflicted with an incurable ailment

[2] Bullen v. Wisconsin, 240 US 625, 60 L Ed 830, 36 S Ct 473 (1916).

at the time of making the transfer without knowledge of its existence. However, he had been informed by his physician of his having an incurable ailment and that his days were numbered, after which a transfer of his property was made either outright or by means of testamentary, the gift, concluded the court, would be in contemplation of death. The property, therefore, must be included in the gross estate for tax purposes.

Intervening Period

Circumstances will often indicate to a reasonable person whether the period of time between one's transferring of property and his death established the fact that the transfer was made in contemplation of death. The shorter the intervening time, of course, the more definite will be the presumption of death as the real motive for the act. The Supreme Court[3] confessed that the time between the making of a transfer of property and death was only circumstantial evidence; and even though there was a lapse of time extending over many years, it was possible to show that the gift was made in contemplation of death.

Whenever a donor dies within two years following the time of making a gift, a reasonable presumption can usually be drawn that the transfer was made in contemplation of death; while if death comes to the donor two years after his making the gift, the conclusion would be just the reverse. Again, such reasoning represents only circumstantial evidence and not conclusive evidence. Whenever a gift is made longer than two years preceding the death of the donor, the burden falls on the Department of Taxation to show that the gift was made in contemplation of death; but if the transfer had been made within the two-year statute, the defenders of the transfer would have the responsibility of showing it was not made in contemplation of death.

The transferor can help to eliminate debatable presumptions by way of making the purpose of the transfer crystal clear, thereby eliminating confusion or misunderstanding. The transferor should be alerted as to the possibilities of questions which might be raised by interested parties after his death concerning the legality of certain transfers of property and also the motives responsible for such decisions.

---

[3] Bullen v. Wisconsin, 240 US 625, 60 L Ed 830, 36 S Ct 473 (1916).

Physical Alertness

In determining the purpose for making gifts, it is important in some situations to consider the age and physical condition of the donor at the time of making the transfer. In the case of a lady 77 years of age who made a transfer of property to her children three years prior to her death, the Commissioner added to her gross estate for tax purposes the transfers to her children claiming that they were made "without an adequate and full consideration in money or money's worth." The court, nevertheless, held that the gifts were not made in contemplation of death in accordance with the estate tax statute.

The age of the donor becomes an important factor for tax purposes when an elderly person dies within two years following his making a transfer of his property. An 85 year-old person gave practically all of his estate to his son and daughter within two years of his death. The court concluded that the transfer was taxable because the gift was made in contemplation of death.[4] In a similar situation, a donor of property was afflicted with an organic ailment and made a gift within two years preceding his death. The transfer was considered a gift in contemplation of death and taxable.[5]

Inter Vivos Gifts

A gift inter vivos is subject to death taxes when the facts reveal that at the time of making the transfer, death of the transferor was impending. Hence, one could only conclude that the gift was made in contemplation of death and that the donor was concerned in protecting his estate from becoming depleted as a result of death taxes. In addition to the gross estate of the deceased representing property owned at his death, the gross estate will also include certain inter vivos transfers made in contemplation of death.

In some jurisdictions that observe the principle of paying the inheritance tax out of the residue of the estate, in the absence of any provision to the contrary, the principle is applied likewise to certain inter vivos gifts. Where the apportionment principle of prorating the tax among the transferees is observed, the

---

[4] Updike v. Com. Int. Reve., (CCA 8), 88F (2d) 807 (1937).

[5] Flack v. Holtegal (cca 7), 93 F 2d 512 (1937).

beneficiaries of the inter vivos gift will be responsible for the payment of the inheritance tax.

One may reasonably presume that an owner of property might wish to pretend to transfer ownership of his property so as to gain a tax advantage at the time of his death and, meanwhile, exercise control over the property during his lifetime. This practice does not fulfill the requirements of an outright gift which constitutes a severing of all rights of ownership and control over the property.

To offset the tendency of property owners to escape having to pay federal death taxes by means of misleading and deceptive practices, Congress recognized the need of a federal gift tax statute in order to control the revenue which was being lost as a result of gifts. This was one successful way of plugging up loopholes in the tax structure. In some instances, states have passed similar laws as a safeguard against losses of revenue.

Whenever an inter vivos gift is included in one's will as representing a share of the estate which is intended for a particular transferee, a question is raised to determine whether such a portion of the estate should be included in the gross estate for tax purposes. It is easily understood that if the transferor had relinquished all of his right to the property, there would have been no cause for including it in the testator's will. Courts have contended that such trusts must share in the apportionment of the tax burden in considering the trust as being incomplete and more of an advancement rather than an outright gift with no conditions involved in the transfer.

Questions of Fact

In determining if a gift is made in contemplation of death, it becomes a question of fact to be determined by a jury. In the event the property in controversy had been completely disposed of free of any reservations by the donor, it would not be considered a subject of the federal estate tax. Where an aged father made outright gifts to his children prior to his plan to remarry, the transfer could not be interpreted as a gift in contemplation of death, and thus would not be subject to the estate tax law. On the other hand, if the transferor had provided for the transferee's realizing no pleasure for such ownership until after the death of the donor, the gift would be included in the gross estate for federal estate tax purposes.

Whenever more than one inter vivos transfers are made, only

those conveyances in contemplation of death are taxable. Courts consider each transfer of property on its individual merits in determining when the estate tax law will apply in each case.

Transfers Within Two Years (Federal, Three Years)

Prior to the passage of the 1976 TAX REFORM ACT, it was provided in the Federal Code that whenever death occurred to the donor within a period of three years following the making of such a transfer of property, the taxpayer had to be able to prove that such a gift was made in contemplation of continued life; otherwise, the conclusion would be that the gift was made in contemplation of dying thereby subjecting the estate of the deceased to the federal estate tax. Such a controversial statute has been made absolutely clear in the TAX REFORM ACT which states that should death occur to the donor within a period of three years following his making a gift of property, the transfer is subject to the gift tax regardless as to whether or not the transfer was made in contemplation of death.

Even though many state statutes provide that property transferred within a period of two years (presently, federal three years) was made in contemplation of death, nevertheless, this presumption can be rebutted by parties having a vested interest in the estate. The state courts have the burden of proof for showing that transfers prior to the death of the deceased were made in contemplation of death in order to justify the subjecting of the estate to the inheritance tax statute.

Transfers Longer Than Two Years (Federal, Three Years)

In the case of a mother who made gifts to her children more than two years prior to her death, the presumption was that the gifts were not made in contemplation of death and that the gifts were not intended for defeating the payment of estate taxes.[6]

State statutes are inclined to observe the two-year period. Section 5731.02 of the Ohio Revised Probate Code states: "As to transfers made more than two years before death, the burden of proof is upon the Department of Taxation to prove that such gifts were made in contemplation of death." Also: "A transfer made in contemplation of death is taxable even though it takes effect prior to the death of the transferor and is irrevocable."

---

[6] Dierks v. United States (DC Kan), 86 F Supp 832 (1949).

Meaning: Contemplation of Death

The term contemplation of death is a relative expression and cannot be defined with exactness. Various circumstances will influence a conclusion as to what the transferor had in mind when making the transfer. An intelligible construction could not be given by merely referring to death which eventually comes to every one, but rather to impending death. In other words, the circumstances must be such as to cause an owner of considerable property to entertain the belief of his approaching death which sparked the urge to dispose of certain property so as to lower the death taxes which would be imposed against his estate at death.

The Supreme Court[7] explains that contemplation of death does not necessarily mean imminent death. One might be young and in the best of health; but while entertaining a negative viewpoint as to what might happen to his estate should he die suddenly, he makes a transfer of his property. Such action would be interpreted by the court as a gift in contemplation of death.

Distinction as to Gifts

The difference between a gift inter vivos and a gift causa mortis is that the former is absolute and irrevocable, while a gift causa mortis is a gift in contemplation of impending death and reserving the power of revocation. In either event, the property must be transferred; and the jury is faced with a question of fact as to whether the property involved represents an absolute gift or a conveyance in contemplation of death.

A gift in contemplation of death may closely resemble a gift inter vivos, but the difference is to be found in the transferor's motive. Death must be contemplated when it furnishes the motive for a testamentary disposition. Following the ruling of the Commissioner of Internal Revenue that gifts were made in contemplation of death or they were made without adequate consideration in money or money's worth and thus should be included in the gross estate for tax purposes, the burden of proof falls on the plaintiff to show that the contention of the Commissioner was erroneous and that the estate is entitled to a tax refund.

A mere promise to subsequently make a gift cannot be

[7] Allen. Col. of Int. Rev. v. Trust Company of Georgia, 326 US 630, 90 L Ed 367, 66 S Ct 389 (1946).

enforced, since the promise is gratuitous; but after the transfer has been made, nothing can be done to have the gift rescinded. An actual transfer results from a physical relinquishment of the ownership and possession of the property. A constructive transfer of property is the surrender of something as a token of ownership, such as a warehouse receipt, a bill of lading, a key to one's jewelry box, automobile, or his business establishment.

When a transfer of property is testamentary, the testator may wish that the distribution of the property to his designated beneficiaries be made immediately following his death. If the testator desires to have the transfer withheld until some future time following his death, he should name a trustee to whom the title will vest for the benefit of a remainderman who will receive the ownership to the property after the lapse of a stated period of time or following the happening of a specified contingency.

Tax Savings

Courts are placed on the defensive in concluding if gifts are made in contemplation of death. There exists an urge on the part of a property owner to legally escape estate and succession taxes against property which he gives away, thus avoiding the listing of such property in the decedent's gross estate for tax purposes at his death. He entertains the opinion that property which he gives away should not be listed in his gross estate at death. Even though the transferor was in poor health and believed death was approaching, this fact alone, claimed the court, would not justify a conclusion that the gift was made in contemplation of death.[8]

It goes without saying that the donor has personal reasons for making donations of property, but probably the main concern is to escape inheritance and estate taxes. To accomplish this objective, various requirements must be observed:

(a) The transfer must not be made in contemplation of death.

(b) Consideration given in return for the transfer must be adequate and in money or money's worth.

(c) A living trust must be irrevocable and without the trustor's right to revoke, alter, or change the terms of the trust.

---

[8] Allen, Col. of Int. Rev. v. Trust Company of Georgia, 326 US 630, 90 L Ed 367, 66 S Ct 389 (1946).

(d) Neither the principal nor the interest may subsequently vest in the trustor.

(e) The trustor cannot reserve the right of control over the administration of the trust.

The estate tax and the gift tax are closely related in purpose and accomplishment. In fact, the federal gift tax is intended to supplement the federal estate tax and to prevent the escape of revenue through inter vivos gifts. This principle was emphasized in a court decision[9] where the creator of a trust reserved the power to alter the disposition, in the future, of the designated property. Hence, the transfer was subjected to the estate tax since it resembled a revocable trust.

In the state of New Jersey, the decedent, while seemingly in good health, transferred property to his wife within a month prior to his death. The court ruled that the transfer was in contemplation of death and should necessarily be included in the decedent's gross estate for tax purposes.

Determining Tax Applicable

In order that a transfer of property may be exempt from the estate tax, there must be an irrevocable assignment of ownership. In the absence of a state statute declaring otherwise, the state inheritance tax cannot be evaded by one's maintaining the right to the income, profit, or control over the property until his death. The trust instrument prepared by the trustor, in the case of Spiegel v. Commissioner[10], provided that the income was to be paid to his three children; and should the children precede the trustor in death, the income was to be distributed to their issues, if any; otherwise, the income was to go to the creator's other children. Following the death of the creator, the corpus was to be divided in the same manner. However, no provision was made for the distribution of the corpus should the creator survive his children or his children's issues. The majority of the judges held that the trust property should be included in the trustor's gross estate for tax purposes, since the Internal Revenue Code included property transferred during one's lifetime and "intended to take effect in possession or enjoyment at or after his death."

---

9 Hesslein v. Hoey, (CCA 2), 91 F 2d 954 (1937).

10 335 US 701, 93 L Ed 330, 69 S Ct 301 (1948).

The *Ohio Probate Law* makes a very clear summary as to the meaning of "contemplation of death." "The controlling test as to whether a given distribution is in contemplation of death is dependent upon the motive or purpose of the transferor. If it concerns an act of generosity or kindness or to relieve the needs of the donee, or if in appreciation of or a reward for services rendered, the transfer is not taxable; but if the motive or purpose is to achieve a distribution at death, each case must be determined by an examination of the facts and circumstances existing at the time of the transfer."

The basic taxing principles involved in transferring the title of property to become effective at the time of death of the testator or in contemplation of death involve a tax consideration on the conveyance of the estate, as well as on the privilege of receiving the property. The ownership is transferred from the deceased to living individuals; and the estate of the deceased will be responsible for the payment of the estate tax, while the devisees and legatees must share their pro-rata portions of the inheritance tax unless the statute or the testator provides for such payments out of the residue of the estate.

Chapter 17

Tax Regulations

Not only does the federal government impose an estate tax at the time of death on property possessed by the deceased, but states also have statutes known as inheritance, succession, or legacy and succession tax. The main consideration of federal and state tax regulations is that of determining the exact property against which the various death taxes will apply. Because of the numerous ways available for making possible the escaping of death taxes, particularly through inter vivos gifts, the federal government, and to some extent the state governments, are giving more attention to the necessity for statutes regulating gifts between living persons.

State Tax Similarities

The inheritance tax statutes in the different states have a striking resemblance to the federal statute. Their general basic principles, of course, are similar. While the inheritance tax statutes indicate slight variations, they come near being approximately the same. In addition to the state inheritance taxes, some states have patterned after the federal government in having an estate tax which is levied against the gross estate rather than the inheritances.

In view of the fact that the federal government prohibits the states from imposing a tax on United States bonds, the question of controversy by the states concerns whether such bonds might be taxable under the state inheritance tax laws. The Supreme Court of Tennessee[1] ruled that the state's inheritance tax statute was a privilege tax on the right of inheriting property under the inheritance laws of the state.

---

[1] 186 Tenn 228, 209 SW 2d 47, 47 ALR 2d 1012 (1948).

The executor in the state of Washington[2] listed the United States Treasury Bonds of the deceased in the federal estate tax return at their par value. The court contended that the bonds should have been listed at their fair market value.

In a much earlier New York[3] decision, the court explained that while there were state tax exemptions on United States bonds, there was not a violation of the federal statute in considering the bonds as part of the taxable estate for determining the state inheritance tax.

An early Pennsylvania[4] ruling recognized the right of the state to collect an inheritance tax on bonds. The court contended that the state inheritance tax was levied on the administration of an estate; and to refuse the state the right to include United States bonds in the taxable estate would interfere with the proper administration of the estate of a deceased.

The Supreme Court of Montana[5] concluded that the value of United States Treasury Bonds for determining the federal estate tax was the market value on the day of the owner's death and not according to the face value.

Privilege Tax

One source of income for both the federal and state governments is derived from taxes imposed on the estates of deceased persons. Unless otherwise stipulated in the testator's will, the inheritance tax will be collected from the various legatees and devisees in return for their rights to receive the property. The federal estate tax is levied against the entire taxable estate, and is referred to as a privilege tax for the testator in return for his right to designate the beneficiaries who will share in his estate.

States which have an estate tax statute, in addition to the inheritance tax, follow the procedure of the federal government in basing the tax on the net taxable estate. Thus, in those states which have both the inheritance and estate tax laws, the inheritance tax will be paid by the beneficiaries, while the estate tax will be assessed against the taxable estate.

Surviving Spouse

The widow has the right under state law to take according to her husband's will or to renounce such a right in electing to take against the will in accordance to her legal option. The fed-

---

[2] Eggert v. State of Washington, respondent, 510 P 2d 645 (1973).

[3] Re Guigg's Estate, 15 NYS 548, 47 ALR 2d 1013 (1891).

[4] 52 Pa 181 (1866).

[5] State Board of Equalization of Montana v. Estate of Powers 676 P 2d 506 (1970).

eral estate tax on the taxable estate will be considerably larger since the widow will be ineligible for marital deduction when she elects to take under the law. Proceeds from her husband's life insurance policies in which she is named the beneficiary will not be subject to the estate tax.

Should the particular jurisdiction, or the will itself, provide that the inheritance tax will be paid out of the residue of the estate instead of being apportioned, the widow, in electing to take under the law, will suffer a disadvantage because the gross taxable estate, after the payment of debts and funeral expenses, will be larger resulting in higher estate tax.

The 1976 TAX REFORM ACT makes some radical changes in the estate and gift taxes as applied to the surviving spouse who can elect to take one-half of the adjusted gross estate or $250,000, whichever is the larger. Thus, marital deduction allows a larger amount for estates smaller than an adjusted gross estate of $500,000, since fifty per cent of the adjusted gross estate would equal the $250,000 allowance. When the gross taxable estate exceeds $500,000, the law favors the large estate. For instance, if the adjusted gross estate, under the old law, amounted to $400,000, the maximum marital deduction of fifty percent would be $200,000, while under the new law, the deduction of fifty per cent or $250,000, whichever is the larger, would come to $250,000.

Gifts to one's spouse under the old law were not taxable to the extent of one-half of the gross taxable estate. After December 31, 1976, the first $100,000 is not taxable, with no marital deduction allowance from $100,000 to $200,000, and a deduction of fifty per cent of the gross taxable estate in excess of $200,000.

Sources of Responsibility

The executor or administrator will be responsible for the payment of the federal estate and the state inheritance taxes. The manner in which the taxes are to be apportioned will have to be in accordance with the law of the particular jurisdiction. A New York statute, for example, provided that unless otherwise specified in the will as to how the federal death tax was to be paid by the executor or administrator, it was to be implied that the tax was to be apportioned among the distributees or beneficiaries of the estate.

The United States District Court[6] recognized the Wisconsin statute which provided that whenever the provisions set forth

[6] Green, Executrix v. United States, 336 F Supp 464 (1971).

in the will for paying taxes, debts, and other expenses of the deceased, do not provide sufficient funds, that portion of the estate not disposed of under the terms of the will should be the first to be appropriated for this purpose. The widow was concerned in not taking under the will, thereby shifting the payment of the taxes, debts, and other expenses of the deceased to the residuary. This resulted in the widow's being unable to claim marital deduction free of taxes, debts, and other expenses of the estate.

The deceased in the state of Connecticut[7] left a sizeable estate with $45,000 designated for a number of charities. The executor claimed a charitable deduction of only $30,000 because the residue, out of which the taxes were to be paid, was insufficient. The residue deficiency was prorated over the various charitable bequests, as well as the general legacies. Later the executor maintained that the estate was entitled to the full $45,000 deduction since the Connecticut statute clearly stated that the tax burden was to be prorated unless the testator's will indicated otherwise. The executor was unsuccessful in his request for such a deduction for the full amount of the charitable bequest because of the insufficient amount in the residue which made necessary the payment of the excess taxes in accordance with the statutory provision.

Deductible Claims

The *1954 Internal Revenue Code* lists certain deductions which are to be made from the gross estate of the deceased, such as funeral expenses, expenses incurred in the administration of the estate, claims of creditors, and liens against the estate in the form of unpaid mortgages on the property included in the gross estate. The court, in Old Colony Trust Company v. Malley,[8] explained that the property which is subject to tax is the gross estate of the deceased less the allowed deductions for debts, expenses, and charges against the estate.

Just what is meant by deduction claims against the estate of the deceased for inheritance tax purposes is not too well established. In a Maryland[9] court decision, a problem facing the court concerned whether a claim against the estate was deductible even though it had not been paid. The claim against the estate by creditors amounted to more than one million dollars, but the executor was able to pay less than one-half of that

[7] Mosher v. United States, 390 F Supp 1041 (1975).

[8] (CCA 1), 15 F 2d 105 (1926).

[9] Baer v. Milbourne, (DC-Md), 13 F Supp 998 (1936).

amount. The Commissioner ruled that only the amount of the debt which had been paid could be claimed as a deduction against the estate. The court, however, ruled that all enforceable claims against the estate are deductible despite the fact that they are not paid.

The 1976 TAX REFORM ACT provides that should the heir of a deceased transfer or sell the property to a nonfamily party within fifteen years following the death of the deceased, and the property is not used for farming or as a closely-held business, the estate tax on such portion of the estate can be recaptured in full during the first ten years. Between the tenth and fifteenth years, the recapture becomes a distribution according to a monthly plan.

Supporting Evidence

One who has paid a federal estate tax and wishes to recover the disbursement has the burden of proof to show that the gift was not made in contemplation of death. A tax deficiency was claimed by the Collector of Internal Revenue because of gifts which had been made in contemplation of death. It was the responsibility of the appellant to prove that the transfer was not made in contemplation of death. This the appellant was unable to do, and the deduction assessed by the Commissioner was affirmed by the United States Court of Appeals.[10]

It is not essential for a claim to be presented to the Probate Court for determining the estate tax, but a decree by such court favoring the claim is evidence of deductibility. The United States District Court contended that the payment of attorney fees in endeavoring to have removed a derelict guardian nominated by the testator was deductible in establishing the net taxable estate for estate tax purposes.

When a living trust is created, it might be considered an inter vivos or a trust in contemplation of death. The ruling of the Supreme Court[11] was that the trust estate is subject to the succession tax at the time the trust was created in contemplation of death.

---

[10] Erickson v. Smith (DC Cal), 108 F Supp 412 (1952).

[11] Guggenhein v. Com. of Int. Rev. 314 US 621, 86 L Ed 499, 62 S Ct

Chapter 18

Gross Estate Evaluation

Just what constitutes the gross estate of the deceased is clearly defined in the *1954 Internal Revenue Code*: "The value of the gross estate shall include the value of all property (except real property situated outside of the United States) to the extent of any interest therein at which the decedent has at any time made a transfer (except in case of a bona fide sale for an adequate and full consideration in money or money's worth), by trust or otherwise, under which he has retained for his life or for any period not ascertainable without reference to his death or for any period which does not, in fact, end before his death."[1]

As to the time of making the transfer, the *Internal Revenue Code* further states: "If the deceased within a period of three years ending with the date of his death (except in case of a bona fide sale for an adequate and full consideration in money or money's worth) transferred an interest in property, relinquished a power, or exercised or released a general power of appointment, such transfer, relinquishment, exercise, or release shall, unless shown to the contrary, be deemed to have been made in contemplation of death within the meaning of this section (relating to revocable transfers and powers of appointment); but no such transfer, relinquishment, exercise, or release made before such three-year period shall be treated as having been made in contemplation of death."[2]

---

[1] 1954 Internal Revenue Act, Section 2036.
[2] 1954 Internal Revenue Act, Section 2035.

Estate Tax Deductions

The gross estate represents the total value of the ownership at the time of the decedent's death. The value of the property which will be subject to the estate tax will involve the listing of a number of deductions, including:

(a) The $60,000 standard exemption in determining the federal estate tax under the old law has been changed to a tax credit of $30,000 for the year 1977 with larger phased-in credit each year through 1981. The $30,000 credit is equivalent to an exemption of $120,000.

(b) Funeral expenses, including burial expense such as undertaker cost, ministerial fee, burial lot, and cost of monument.

(c) Administrative expenses covering court costs, attorney fees, executor or administrator fees, and fees of appraisers.

(d) Accrued expenses against the estate at the time of the decedent's death, such as property tax, and tax on earned income.

(e) Claims of creditors for personal debts of the decedent at the time of his death.

(f) Marital deduction under the old law allowed the surviving spouse a deduction to the extent of fifty per cent of the gross taxable estate; but the 1976 TAX REFORM ACT increases the allowance to a maximum of $250,000 or fifty per cent of the gross taxable estate, whichever is the larger.

(g) Gifts for charitable, educational, religious, or scientific causes.

Evaluating Estate for Tax Purposes

The federal estate tax is described as a tax on all of the taxable property of the deceased; and, as such, it is interpreted as a privilege for the transmission of one's estate, rather than a privilege of beneficiaries for receiving all of the estate or portions thereof. The transfer of the estate involves the exercise of legal power of relinquishing the ownership over property, while the inheritance pertains to the privilege of succession. Whenever the debts of the deceased exceed the value of the estate and the proceeds of life insurance payable to the estate, no tax is to be paid.[3]

Many factors have to be taken into consideration by the court in determining the value to be included in the gross estate for inheritance tax purposes. In determining the value of real estate, for example, courts have observed various factors, such as: location, nature of the property, its comparative value in the particular locality, returns from rent, and income from property sales in the particular area during the past year of comparable property.

The testator should distinguish between the debts and obligations of the estate which must be paid and charged against the beneficiaries for federal estate and state inheritance taxes. In the absence of clear instructions in the testator's will as to the payment of just debts, funeral expenses, and the cost of administration, after which the dividing of the estate according to a definite plan, such procedure must naturally be implied as to the testator's intention.

It is obvious that the estate will be responsible for the payment of all legal charges against it, and the necessary provision can quite conveniently be designated in the will for the payment of both federal and state taxes. Arrangements can also be indicated for the payment of taxes on real property in which a beneficiary has a life estate or taxes on real estate which is intended for sale in the near future. Also, if a profitable business is to be held in trust, its anticipated taxes can be accounted for even though the income therefrom might be intended for some charitable, religious, or educational cause.

Tax Based on Time of Death

The estate of the deceased, which will be subject to the estate tax at the time of the testator's death, will include all property of which he was possessed at the time of death, except real property located in a foreign country. This degree of ownership includes trusts which have been created in contemplation of death and property in which the testator has reserved a life interest or had reserved the right to revoke.

The federal estate tax is levied against the gross taxable estate of the deceased who was a citizen or a resident of the United States.[4] Courts are not in agreement as to the tax regulation to be observed in view of changes in tax rates which are taking place

[3] Helvering v. Northwestern National Bank & Trust Co., (CCA 8), 89 F (2d) 553 (1937).

[4] Goodman v. Granger, 355 US 835, 2 L Ed 2d 47, 78 S Ct 57 (1957).

from time to time. Some courts take the position that the legislature intended that the law in effect at the time the transferor died was to be applied. No doubt, this precedent would be simplest to follow. Other courts, however, contend that the rates in effect when the transfer was made should be the basis for determining the tax.

As to the price for listing United States Treasury Bonds of the deceased, following his death, for determining the amount of the state inheritance tax, the Illinois[5] court explained that the price which the owner could have expected to receive for the bonds and the buyer was willing to pay, as indicated in the market quotation on the date of the owner's death, was the accepted value and not the face value of the bonds.

Tax-Free Bequests

Special tax-free bequests were made in a will with the remainder going to a named beneficiary after the payment of the cost of administration, court costs, and taxes. A Colorado[6] court ruled that the term taxes included the inheritance tax which was to be paid out of the residue of the estate, after which the remainder of the estate was to go to the general beneficiary described in the will of the testator.

Should the testator provide in his will that a particular debtor was to be released of a certain financial obligation, this would be equivalent to the bequeath of a legacy in the will. After all, there could be no difference in transferring the subject matter after the death of the legator and the making of an outright gift. In either case, the federal estate and the state inheritance taxes would apply.

Uniformity of Inheritance Taxes

Inheritance taxes in the various states are not expected to be in complete uniformity. Yet, should there be too much variation in the tax structure in the different states, there might develop a strong incentive for an individual's preferring one state over another in choosing his place of domicile. The law of some states allow a deduction of federal estate tax, while in other states, a contrary rule is adopted. In some jurisdictions, property inherited, which is subject to the state inheritance tax, is pro-rated according to all heirs alike; and in other states, exemp-

[5] Voss, Appellee v. First Nat'l Bank of Rock Island, Appellant 5 Ill App 3rd 320 (1973).

[6] Bourquin's Estate, 87 Colo 144, 37 ALR 2d 123 (1930).

tions are allowed according to closeness of kin. Some states have observed a rather strict policy of having a tax schedule as near as possible in conformity with the tax structures of other states.

Subject to Inheritance Tax

The inheritance tax is not confined merely to a levy against ownership of property described under the common law. An Ohio decision defines property subject to the inheritance tax as that which was held by the decedent at the time of his death or transferred by him in contemplation of death. Courts are also inclined to look to the economic interests of the deceased as well as to his actual ownership. An Illinois[7] court rúled that the inheritance tax did not include the income accruing after the decedent's death.

In order to escape the inheritance tax, it perhaps is sometimes tempting to list deductions for services rendered by members of the family. A court in Illinois[8] contended that when no consideration is mentioned for such services, there can be no escape from the state inheritance tax. To hold otherwise, claimed the court, would naturally lead to numerous claims and complications.

Determining Value of Securities

The court will be responsible for agreeing as to the proper value of listed securities for tax purposes. There is a strong possibility of the Commissioner's setting the price too high. This tendency can be somewhat overcome by way of a promise of a potential purchaser of the securities at a stated price. If the subject of the gift consists of stocks and bonds, and there is a market for such securities, the median price at which such securities were sold on a particular date can be determined the fair market price. Whenever the securities in question are listed on a stock exchange, the matter of establishing the value of a particular gift becomes quite simple by way of discovering the median average of the highest and lowest price at which the securities were sold on the particular date or the nearest date possible.

In the case of corporate securities, the value will be the market value of listed securities on the day of the decedent's

[7] Fernandez v. Wiemer, 326 US 340, 90 L Ed 116, 66 S Ct 178 (1945).

[8] People v. Porter, 287 Ill 401, 123 NE 59, 7 ALR 1041 (1919).

death. Where securities are not listed on an exchange, the value will have to be determined by a comparison with listed securities of corporations which are identical or similar as to operational functions.

The value of other property which was transferred as a gift would be the market value determined by the price the vendee was willing to give and the vendor was willing to receive in return for his goods. In other words, it represents the price at which the minds of the two contracting parties were in agreement.

Ownership of Non-Residents

The federal gift tax, as outlined in the *1954 Internal Revenue Code*, applies to all gifts of property, regardless of location, made by residents, as well as citizens, of the United States. As to gifts by non-resident aliens, the property is taxed if located within the United States. The only exemptions which can be claimed by the non-resident alien include property located in a foreign country; but this exception does not apply when the non-resident alien removed the property to a foreign country after which the gift was made.

Stock of domestic corporations held by non-resident aliens is recognized as property located in the United States, insofar as the federal estate tax is concerned. Thus, the law applies only to stock of domestic corporations. Prior to the passage of the *1954 Internal Revenue Code*, the law included the ownership of stock in foreign corporations held by such parties whenever the certificate was located in the United States; but this provision of the law has been removed.

At the death of a non-resident who is not a citizen of the United States, certain types of property located in the United States will be included in his gross estate and subject to the estate tax. The *Federal Code (Annotated)*[9] defines such types of ownership as follows:

(a) Stock held in domestic corporations.
(b) Revocable transfers (whether by trust or otherwise) of property located in the United States.
(c) Deposits in banks located in the United States.
(d) Shares of stock and bonds in foreign corporations but deposited with domestic banks for collecting the income and for making transfers in contemplation of death.

The Federal Code also lists the various types of property

[9] Title 26, Section 2101.

held by non-resident aliens which are not taxable:

(a) Stocks and bonds held in foreign corporations.
(b) Proceeds of life insurance issued by foreign companies.
(c) Deposits with a party engaged in the banking business for non-residents not citizens of the United States.
(d) Works of art imported by a non-resident for exhibition purposes or loaned to a public museum.

Gifts With Reservations

The *1954 Internal Revenue Code*[10] includes in the gross estate for tax purposes any property transfers (other than a bona fide sale for full and valuable consideration in money or money's worth), including a trust or otherwise, where the transferor has retained an estate for life or for a period which can be ascertained only in terms of one's death.

An action was brought in Pennsylvania[11] to obtain a tax refund for taxes paid under the 1918 Revenue Act. The creator was to have possession and enjoyment of the property during her lifetime. The court contended that the deceased conveyed property with a reservation of a life estate to herself which amounted to a post-mortem disposition of property, the possession of which being withheld until the death of the grantor, at which time it was to be included in the gross estate of the deceased for tax purposes.

Transfers for Consideration

At the time of the testator's death, the big problem is that of determining that portion of the estate which will be subject to tax. Such property will include not only the estate of the deceased at the time of death and transfers made in contemplation of death, but also transfers which were made for inadequate consideration.

Whenever the conveyance is made in good faith and the parties acted adversely, the price received by the vendor will constitute the best price obtainable under the circumstances and would not be subject to the gift tax. Should property be donated soon after it was acquired, the cost price would be the basis for determining the value of property for gift tax purposes.[12]

---

[10] Section 2036.

[11] McCaughn v. Girard Trust Co., (CCA 3), 11 F 2d 520 (1926).

[12] Guggenheim v. Rasquin, 312 US 254, 85 L Ed 813, 61 S Ct 507 (1941).

When an interest or right in property is relinquished in a sale transaction which is not a bona fide transfer for adequate consideration in money's worth, the amount to be included in the gross estate of the deceased will be the difference in the fair market value at the time of the decedent's death and the amount received for the transfer. The application of the principle is obviously intended to discourage a person who might be lying at death's door from giving away his property freely in return for a minimum of consideration so as to lower the value of his estate which will be subject to tax.

Basis for Gift Tax

A gift tax shall be imposed on any transfer of property, whether by a resident or a non-resident, except in the case of intangible property by one who is a non-resident, not a citizen of the United States, and in no way engaged in business in the United States during the calendar year in which the gift is made. In considering the various taxes, the objective in planning an estate is either to consider the advisability of making gifts of property while living or to have such property included in the gross estate for tax purposes at the testator's death.

When the donor gives away his property, he is depriving himself of the pleasure and enjoyment of it during the remainder of his life. If he prefers leaving it for his heirs following his death, the estate tax and the inheritance tax will take a portion of the estate. Thus, one should observe several plans of procedure before deciding which would be most desirable and economically sound for himself, as well as his heirs to whom his estate will eventually be devised and bequeathed.

When property is given outright to another, the basis for determining the value is the fair market value at the time of making the gift. Under some circumstances, the gift of certain property, such as heirlooms and valuable paintings, may be given to charitable organizations for which large deductions can be realized. While the property might be appraised at a very high rate, yet, the owner, in all probability, would have to search for a long time before finding a prospect who would be ready and willing to pay the appraised price. In the event property is sold to an heir, particularly just a short time before the vendor's death, the circumstances might raise a presumption by the Commissioner of Internal Revenue that a collusion had been entered into, since the consideration transferred was not adequate, thereby necessitating the listing for gift tax purposes the difference in the amount of consideration given for the property and its fair market value.

Chapter 19

Motives for Gifts

In order to constitute a gift of property, there must be an actual transfer of ownership. The mere promise to make a gift is considered by the courts as being gratuitous and representing no legal significance. The expression of an intention to make a gift at a later time signifies only a moral obligation which cannot be enforced.

Trust or Otherwise

Except in cases of transfers of property for adequate and full consideration in money or money's worth, all such conveyances, whether by trust or otherwise, or in contemplation of imminent death, shall be included in the gross estate subject to the estate tax. In the event the deceased had transferred his interest in certain property within a period of three years preceding his death or relinquished his reserved power of appointment, the incident will be interpreted, unless shown to the contrary, as if the transfer had been made in contemplation of death.

States have invoked similar tax regulations on successions or inheritances, whether by trusts or outright gifts according to declarations in a will or by intestate inheritance. Even though a transfer of property is made by gift, sale, deed, or grant for less than full or adequate consideration in money or money's worth, whether in contemplation of death or to become effective at the transferor's death, will be subject to the inheritance or succession tax.

Proper planning for skipping estate tax payments during one or more generations in a carefully-drawn instrument or in making such trust provisions in one's last will and testament has become quite a popular procedure for thrifty individuals. Congress, meanwhile, has been concerned with limiting the amount that can be transferred in a tax-free trust. The TAX REFORM ACT of 1976 introduced a change in generation-skipping trusts which will affect mainly very large estates. The maximum amount which a trustor can leave in a tax-free trust is $250,000 for each of his children. Provision can be made for the income to go to a child during his lifetime; and following his death, the income will go to the grandchildren for the duration of their lives, after which the corpus may be descended to the trustor's great-grandchildren according to the wishes expressed by the trustor.

Gifts and Irrevocable Trusts

A gift by means of a trust will become subject to the gift tax when there is an abandonment of control over the property to the degree that the trustor has no authority to change, alter, or revoke the trust. In the case of a trustor who reserved such a right and later resigning as trustee and relinquishing all reserved rights, the assumption would be that the gift had been completed and the property involved would become a proper subject of the gift tax.

A father in Pennsylvania[1] created an irrevocable inter vivos trust in favor of his son. Broad discretionary powers were granted to the trustees, and no control was exercised or reserved by the trustor. The trustees were authorized to make all decisions necessary relative to the education, maintenance, and care of the beneficiary. The trust property, according to the court, was not to be included in the father's taxable estate, but would be subject to the gift tax.

Whenever the income from an irrevocable trust, which does not vest in the transferee until after the death of the transferor, results in the enjoyment by the transferee being postponed until following the death of the transferor, the property thereby becomes taxable. An irrevocable trust, without reservations, is subject to the gift tax; and while the donor is primarily responsible for the payment of the tax, the donee and the trustee assumed personal liabilities for its payment.

Promissory notes which were given by a parent in Louisiana[2]

---

[1] McCullough v. Granger (DC Pa), 128 F Supp 611 (1955).

[2] Atkins v. Com. of Int. Rev., (CCA 5), 30 F 2d 761 (1929).

to certain ones of his children to equalize his gifts to them were considered as representing valuable consideration under the law of that state and were regarded as deductible. The Louisiana law was observed by the court at that period, regardless of the findings in other states, while maintaining that there was sufficient consideration for the notes in allowing them to be deducted from the gross estate for tax purposes.

Gift Promises

It is not enough to merely publish one's intention to make a transfer of certain property in the future. To be effective, the promise would necessarily have to be executed. Merely giving a key to one's hope chest while stating that upon the death of the promisor, the title would vest in the promisee, would not be sufficient to constitute a transfer.

In order to bind one to his moral obligation to make a transfer, the donor must make an outright gift and completely depart with his possession and control over the property. Otherwise, the naked promise would carry with it no enforceable legal obligation. An essential element for entering into a binding contract is consideration; and it becomes noticeably lacking in a promise to make a gift in the future and, meanwhile, receiving nothing of value in exchange for such a promise. Whenever a promise fails to be supported by consideration, nothing can be done in the way of securing from the court an order of specific performance or in receiving damages in a court of law because of the promisor's failure to make good his commitment.

Representing Antenuptial Agreement

The *1954 Internal Revenue Code*[3] provides that the agreement of a spouse to relinquish her right of dower in consideration of property transferred to her is deductible against the estate of the transferor, since it is considered a bona fide gift, and the consideration is money or money's worth. Prior to the passage of the Act, the court, in Harris v. Commissioner,[4] contended that property transferred under an antenuptial or postnuptial agreement was deductible to the extent of its fair consideration.

The purpose of the gift tax is to prevent the donor from depleting his estate tax-free through gifts during the donor's

[3] 1954 Internal Revenue Code, Section 2512.
[4] 340 US 106, 95 L Ed Ill, 71 S Ct 18 (1950).

lifetime. The gift tax and the inheritance tax do not include transfers made for an adequate and full consideration in money or money's worth. Hence, a postnuptial property settlement was declared subject to the federal gift tax, and this conclusion was affirmed by the Supreme Court prior to the adoption of the above-mentioned Code provision.

Gift Advantages and Disadvantages

Over a period of time, an owner of property can take advantage of yearly gifts of $3,000 for each of any number of donees without any obligation for the payment of gift taxes. Insofar as future income taxes are concerned, whenever it is income-producing property which is the subject of a transfer, the transferee, most likely, will be in a very low income bracket as compared with a possibly higher tax position of the transferor. At the death of the transferor, the heirs can expect an over-all larger share of the estate, including previous transfers, because of the various tax-exempt gifts which had previously been executed.

Provided gifts are not made in contemplation of death, a donor may adopt a consistent policy of making yearly transfers to his heirs; and over a period of years, he can succeed in liquidating quite a large amount of his estate for which there has been created no tax responsibility. Through careful planning, the owner of an estate can escape definite gift and death taxes.

While the $3,000 yearly gift, or $6,000 if the donor's spouse agrees with such a transfer, is retained in the 1976 TAX REFORM ACT, the $30,000 exemption during the lifetime of the donor, or $60,000 if the spouse signs his or her waiver, have been deleted as exemptions.

Assuming that the donor is willing to relinquish his ownership and control over certain property which has been made the subject of a gift, thereby taking advantage of tax exemptions, there are certain disadvantages which the donor can anticipate. After some donees acquire the ownership of property, their general expressions of appreciation might be lacking. Then, too, there will always exist the possibility of the donees' failure to exercise the proper foresight in caring for the property to the satisfaction of the donor. The donees' attitude of "come easy go easy" might dominate their thinking and actions, resulting in carelessness and extravagance in their exercise of managerial control over the property.

There always exists the probability of a donee's dying prematurely prior to the death of the donor and leaving the donee's estate subject to the payment of death taxes. Even if the donee died testate or intestate, the distribution of the property would, no doubt, be disappointing to the donor. Hence, circumstances naturally alter cases; and it is the responsibility of the owner of property to determine which plan of disposition is to be regarded best for him after carefully weighing the various alternatives. Because of the uncertainty of the donor concerning his making definite conveyances while he is living or postponing the transfers until following his death, consideration needs to be given to certain disadvantages to one's favoring outright gifts:

(a) There is a possibility of the donor's surviving the donee, and, therefore, having to observe a considerable amount of the estate being paid out in the form of estate and inheritance taxes upon the death of the donee.

(b) The donee's incapacity for exercising complete and independent control over the estate.

(c) Possibility of disappointment of the donor in the donee's general attitude following the transfer.

(d) Lack of foresight by the donee for investing and managing the property.

(e) The donee's urge to speculate in the making of investments in an effort to increase the value of the estate at the expense of assuming great risks.

(f) The possibility of the donee's acquiring extravagant ideas as to the use and care of property.

Conditional and Non-Conditional Gifts

State courts, as well as federal courts, have observed the old-established rule of the Supreme Court of declaring the reservation of a beneficial interest in property by the transferor as conditional and subject to the federal and state death taxes. When the conditions in the transfer are such as to deprive the donee of any benefits until following the transferor's death, the courts reason that the transfer was made in contemplation of death and should be included in the gross estate for tax purposes.

If there is a possibility that a gift to charity will not be made because of a condition, it is not deductible. For example, a parent who bequeaths property to a charitable organization provided the donee's child does not leave a bodily heir would be conditional. Also, when one promises to give a definite sum of money to a charitable organization provided the charity can raise a similar amount would be conditional and non-deductible.

In order that a gift may be valid and effective, it is necessary that the owner relinquish all control over the property. In some instances, an attempt may be made to make a gift and gain an exemption while maintaining control over the property. This amounts to an inconsistency which the courts do not look on with favor. Certainly, it would not indicate an act of good faith on the part of the donor; and no tax exemption could be justified.

Present and Future Interests

A gift cannot be excluded from the gross estate for tax purposes if it is for a future interest. The enjoyment of the property by the donee cannot be delayed until the happening of a particular contingency and not represent a future interest. The *1954 Internal Revenue Code* describes gifts, except those involving future interests, as representing assignments which were made during the year 1955 and subsequent years and subject to the gift tax, with the exception of the yearly deduction of $3,000 to each donee and the $30,000 standard exemption.

To justify the deduction of a gift from the gross estate for tax purposes, it is necessary that the gift be irrevocable and that the donor not be privileged to exercise any control over it. Either retaining a life estate in property or transferring only a life estate is taxable at the testator's death. In other words, there must be a relinquishment of all rights over the manner of its subsequent disposal. Merely delaying the donee's use, enjoyment, and possession of the property until some future date can only be interpreted as a future interest. The distinction between a present and a future interest is the postponement of enjoyment, use, and ownership of the property as compared with the present use thereof.

Factors Constituting Gifts

There should be no doubt relative to the donor's intention of making a gift of property. The act must be unequivocal and free of any conditions or contingencies in order to escape the payment of a gift tax. In drawing conclusions as to the motives for making transfers of property, the court will desire to consider such factors as: (1) age of the donor; (2) closeness of kin; (3) conditions of health; (4) the size of the donor's estate; (5) the value of the gift; (6) the attitude of the donee toward the donor; and (7) the intervening time between the transfer and the death of the donor. Nevertheless, when there is lacking any justification for the court's questioning the sound judgment of the donor, the court may naturally refuse to recognize the gift as a deduction.

Should the evidence reveal that the donor, being closely related to the donee, had been observing a procedure of making regular gifts to the donee, the facts would tend to support the theory that the gifts had not been made in contemplation of death. At the decedent's death, the Commissioner of Internal Revenue added additional taxes for gifts made within two years prior to his death as having been made in contemplation of death. The executor requested a refund of the tax on such gifts. The Court of Claims agreed with the executors in denying the Commissioner's request. The facts showed that the decedent, as early as the year 1901, had been making gifts regularly to his children. His reason was to make the transfers while the donor was living so as to be in a position to advise the donees as to how to successfully manage their estates. The court explained that the factors for differentiating between gifts in contemplation of death or otherwise must be determined by the motives for the transfers. The decision of the Court of Claims, in reversing the action by the Commissioner, was affirmed by the Supreme Court.[5]

Reason for Making Gifts

In the state of Missouri,[6] a donor informed the donee of his transferring to him in the form of a gift the content of the envelope, consisting of 25 $1,000 Federal Reserve Bank Notes. The donee was instructed to write on the envelope that the content represented his personal property, after which the envelope was returned to the donor who put it in his safety deposit box where it was to be kept with the right of possession to be enjoyed by him until his death. The court declared the gift was in contemplation of death and should be included in the gross estate for estate tax purposes.

Only personal property can be the subject of a gift causa mortis, and the one qualification of the donor is that he must have testamentary capacity for making such a gift. Gifts inter vivos are more common, and the requirement for making a valid transfer between living persons is contractual capability.

[5] United States v. Wells, 283 US 102, 75 L Ed 867, 51 S Ct 446 (1931).

[6] Wahl v. Sheehan, (DC Mo), 54 F Supp 56 (1944).

Physical Condition Influencing Gifts

In view of the donor's advancing years, it might be an easy problem for his adviser or counselor to persuade him to make inter vivos gifts. Considering the possibility of the donor's lacking in knowledge and understanding, the tendency might be for him to place complete confidence in his adviser in deciding to make inter vivos gifts as suggested to him. As a result, he would be denied the right of acting as a free agent in making transfers of his property. The question of controversy would be whether the adviser merely explained the situation of making gifts to him personally or whether he unduly influenced the donor to make definite transfers of property. The age of the donor and his physical condition could be important factors for concluding if the gifts were made in contemplation of death.

Courts have established reasonable and acceptable precedents for concluding that just because a person is young and vigorous does not necessarily follow that he will be quite concerned in avoiding taxes as might be expected of an elderly and feeble person. Nevertheless, this presumption can be rebutted, as it would not necessarily imply that gifts in all circumstances will be made in contemplation of death.

Types of Transfers

Statutes subjecting property transferred in contemplation of death to estate and inheritance taxes have been upheld by the courts.[7] Even though the law is well settled that a gift causa mortis is subject to estate and succession taxes, it is also recognized that certain inter vivos gifts, which are executed and irrevocable, are subject to such taxes if they were made in contemplation of death.[8]

The court can be expected to consider the matter as to the proportionate amount of the estate which was transferred just prior to the transferor's death. Should most of the property be transferred immediately preceding the donor's death, the court would be justified and responsible for taking a close look as to the motive for the action. Naturally, such condition would warrant quite a convincing presumption that the purpose of making the transfer was mainly that of escaping the death tax burdens against the estate.

When a transfer is made of property to one's closest relatives, the act is not always motivated by a desire to escape taxes;

---

[7] Milliken v. United States, 283 US 15, 75 L Ed 809, 51 S Ct 324 (1934).

[8] United States v. Wells, 283 US 102, 75 L Ed 867, 51 S Ct 446 (1931).

but the basic reason might be to aid and assist such donees to become self-sustaining and financially independent. The difference in the tax brackets of the donees and that of the donor will often be considered as a means of realizing a substantial saving in taxes. Gifts might also be made for educational purposes so as to better equip the donees for lives of more useful service or to prepare them to enter particular businesses or professions.

Adequate Consideration

The gross estate for tax purposes does not include transfers for adequate consideration. An inter vivos transaction must be unconditional and free of any testamentary disposition. Sometimes the testator, while observing the various possibilities of defeating the tax burden, might endeavor to leave a legacy in his will in payment of an existing debt. Such a transfer should necessarily be included in the gross estate of the deceased and subject to tax.

If adequate consideration in money or money's worth is received for property sold, the proceeds are not subject to tax. In other instances, where transfers are made in contemplation of death or the right to revoke is reserved, the property is included in the gross estate of the deceased for tax purposes. If there is a transfer of property in consideration of the promise of the transferee to care for the transferor during his lifetime, this amounts to valuable and adequate consideration and is not subject to tax.

Purpose of Gift Tax

Congress has been vested with power to pass a federal gift tax statute. The *Internal Revenue Code* provides for the filing of a return each year for gifts inter vivos. The purpose of the gift tax statute was to protect the federal revenue which was being lost through the making of certain gifts which were deductible from income tax and also losses in federal estate taxes through inter vivos gifts.

The Supreme Court[9] gave approval to the gift tax statute in contending that the motive for its passage was to prevent one's escaping the payment of death taxes through the making of inter

---

[9] Sanford v. Com. of Int. Rev., 308 US 39, 84 L Ed 20 (1939).

vivos gifts. It was brought out that the federal estate and gift taxes are closely linked together and should necessarily be interpreted in that manner. Prior to the year 1924, when the first gift tax statute was passed, the donor could create an inter vivos trust and reserve the right to change the beneficiaries or to modify the trust.

Following the passage of the gift tax statute in 1924, the decedent withdrew her last remaining right to modify the trust. After the creator's death in 1928, the Commissioner claimed that the gift became subject to the gift tax after the last remaining reservation was removed in 1924. The Supreme Court[10] affirmed this decision.

The *1954 Internal Revenue Code* makes clear the purpose of the gift tax statute: "The gift tax imposed by Section 2501 shall apply whether the transfer is in trust or otherwise, whether the gift is direct or indirect, and whether the property is real or personal, tangible or intangible; but in the case of a non-resident not a citizen of the United States, shall apply to a transfer only if the property is situated within the United States."

Exception to Gift Tax Statute

Courts recognize and enforce gifts which are made in contemplation of death as being included in the gross estate for estate tax purposes. It is the value of the property at the testator's death that is used in making estate tax calculations. If it is income-producing property, the income will have to be included in the donor's income during his lifetime for income tax purposes.

At the time the deceased made gifts of property, in the case of Milliken v. United States,[11] to his children, the *Federal Revenue Act* covered gifts in contemplation of death. Following the making of the gifts, the decedent died, at which time the tax rate had increased over the rate at the time the gifts were made, thereby imposing a higher tax. The Commissioner was successful in assessing the estate for the difference in the rate at the time the gifts were made and the subsequent rate in effect at the transferor's death.

The argument frequently offered against the observance of the

[10] Section 2511 (A).
[11] 283 US 14, 75 L Ed 809 51 S Ct 324 (1930).

new rate was that it violated the "due process" clause as set forth in the Fifth Amendment to the Constitution. This contention was overruled by the court in explaining that the tax was not to be interpreted as an arbitrary act, since the law could not be applied generally to all cases alike, but, instead, the facts of each case must be interpreted separately.

Close Relationships in Taxes

It cannot be overlooked that the gift tax has a close relationship to the estate tax and also to the income tax. Certain inter vivos transfers will be subject to the federal gift tax. Even though other transfers are inter vivos, but made in contemplation of death, they will be liable for the federal estate tax. The law recognizes certain inter vivos gifts, with limitations, as being non-taxable in calculating the gift tax and as deductions from the gross estate for estate tax purposes, as well as a deduction from income in determining the income tax for the particular period.

There are tax advantages in one's making gifts inter vivos of property when the owner considers the law of average in estimating roughly the number of years which he has before him. Should the insured die within the three years from the time of taking out the policy, under *The Revenue Act*, the presumption would be that the policy was taken out in contemplation of death and would be taxable; but this presumption could be rebutted by the taxpayer.

Saving in Taxes

Taxwise, the making of an outright gift of property or the creating of an irrevocable trust will result in a saving in the estate tax at the death of the donor. Granting that a gift tax will have to be paid, yet this will be offset by a saving in estate tax as a result of the gift tax rate amounting to approximately three-fourths of the estate tax. In addition, certain deductions and allowances offer strong incentives to certain property owners to consider making outright inter vivos gifts of some of their property, particularly that which is income-producing.

When the objective in making family gifts of property is to reduce the income tax and later the estate tax, the property with high return potential will often be preferred for making the transfer. The estate tax later will be calculated within a smaller bracket, and the future income from the income-producing property transferred will result in less income tax from year to year which will have to be paid. Furthermore, the possibility of the value of certain property becoming inflated in the future, as well as the anticipated return to show an increase from year to year, should be taken into consideration prior to the making of gifts.

Several objectives can be present for motivating the donor's desire to convey certain property before his death; namely, (1) to improve the station in life of certain donees; (2) to escape having to pay estate taxes on such property at the donor's death; (3) after taking advantage of the gift tax allowances and deductions, the amount paid out in taxes will be less than would otherwise have to be paid at the donor's death.

Particularly when one has a large estate and wishes to take advantage of a big reduction in taxes by way of making large gifts yearly to various parties, a big saving in taxes against one's estate at the time of death is made possible. Since marital deductions are allowed for husband and wife, a husband can give $6,000 each year to his wife (or vice versa) without incurring any gift tax.

Unified Gift and Estate Tax

The estate tax credit in the 1976 TAX REFORM ACT takes the place of the $60,000 exemption under the old law. The ultimate $47,000 credit, which will be the equivalent of $175,000 exemption, will be phased in over a period of five years. Starting January 1, 1977, the estate of every deceased during that particular year will be allowed a credit of $30,000, which will be the equivalent of $120,000 exemption.

Whenever one entertains any thought of making testamentary dispositions of his property, his intention is that they will become effective at the donor's death; or he might have reasons for concluding that the time of his death is rapidly approaching and decides on making the gifts outright in contemplation of death. In the case of the latter, the court has to determine whether the donor made the gifts in contemplation of living or whether he was influenced through certain known symptoms of his limitation of living and made the gifts believing that he was soon to die.

Being aware of the sizeable amount which will be deducted from his estate in the form of taxes at the time of his death, one can be expected to display some concern with taking advantage of every legal possibility of reducing such tax burden to his estate. Because of the vast losses in revenue through gifts, courts have had the problem of determining whether or not certain transfers were inter vivos or were made in contemplation of impending death.

Individuals possessing considerable wealth are usually reluctant about making gifts of their property while they are living; but the possibility of their realizing escapes from taxes against their estates may serve as a strong incentive for their making the decisions to relinquish their right of ownership to certain properties. As a result, they proceed to make gifts to those who will eventually acquire it anyway. Therefore, the problem facing the owner of property consists of one of two alternatives; namely, (1) departing with the ownership and taking advantage of either escaping from having to pay certain taxes or, at least, eventually getting them reduced, or (2) retain the property with the pleasure accompanying its ownership, but ultimately resulting in larger estate taxes to be paid at his death.

One can get a clear conception of the inadequacies and loopholes of early gift tax statutes in considering a Massachusetts[12] case. Property which was conveyed in trust provided for one-half of the income to go to the trustor during her lifetime, while the other one-half was intended for her daughters and the heirs of their bodies. The ruling of the court was that ownership of property which had been completely surrendered would not be subject to the federal estate tax at the trustor's death.

It was also held that the half of which the trustor had been completely divested was not subject to tax as it represented a gift inter vivos. The United States government has no power, said the court, to tax gifts inter vivos unless the transfers were made in contemplation of impending death. Such a precedent made necessary a supplement to the gift tax statute in limiting the amount of tax-free gifts.

---

12 Bradley v. Nichols, Col. of Int. Rev. (DC Mass), 13 F 2d 857 (1926).

Exercising Power of Appointment

The power of appointment being reserved by the trustor resulted in the inclusion of such property in the trustor's estate following her death, in the case of Helvering v. Safe Deposit and Trust Company;[13] but if the power of appointment had been given the beneficiary without the right of revocation by the transferor, the property would not have been included in the estate of the trustor.

When a will provides a life estate in property for a beneficiary who is given the power of appointment, the transfer will be presumed to have been made at the death of the transferor, at which time the state inheritance tax would be imposed as if the property belonged to the transferee. As to the power of a state to tax, in the case of a testamentary trust created in one state and naming a beneficiary (with the power of appointment in another state), the law is not uniform in the various states. Section 5731.05 of the *Ohio Probate Code* states; "Upon the death of a person who has created a power of appointment, if the donee of the power is a non-resident of this state, all the property of the donor which is subject to taxation . . . shall be deemed to be included in the donor's estate and taxed therein."

As to the credit allowed on prior transfers, the *1954 Internal Revenue Code*[14] states: "The tax imposed shall be credited with all or part of the amount of the federal estate tax paid with respect to the transfer of property (including property passing as a result of the exercise or nonexercise of power of appointment) to the decedent by or from a person (herein designated as transferor) who died within ten years before, or within two years after the decedent's death."

[13] 316 US 56, 86 L Ed 1266, 62 S Ct 925, 139 ALR 1513 (1942).
[14] Section 2013.

Chapter 20

Importance of Deductions

One who possesses ownership in property should be familiar with the various ways of bringing about the eventual transfer most satisfactorily and economically. Circumstances might favor a program of relinquishing his rights to property so as to place yearly income in the future in a much lower income tax bracket. The law, therefore, makes possible a gradual transfer of property rights, but this procedure frequently runs contrary to the owner's desire of exercising exclusive control and the maintaining of a feeling of security in his vast ownership.

Another alternative is for the owner of property to sell it rather than make an outright gift, provided the consideration received is just and reasonable. The Controller of Internal Revenue will naturally take a close look at transfers of property (particularly real property, government bonds, and corporate securities) which were executed shortly prior to the death of the transferor. Should the price given for the property not represent a fair and reasonable consideration in money or money's worth, the difference can justifiably be subject to the gift or estate tax.

According to the 1976 TAX REFORM ACT, property passing to an orphan child who has not attained his majority of twenty-one years is deductible from the gross estate of the deceased to the amount of $5,000 times the number of years preceding his attaining his majority. In the event he should be only five years of age at the time, the deduction would amount to $80,000 from the gross estate of the deceased, or sixteen years times $5,000.

Instead of making a complete and unconditional severance of ownership and control over his property, one might choose as another possibility the creation of a trust which will be either revocable or nonrevocable. As a rule, the trustor may wish to experiment with the trust relationship so that in the event it does not prove to be very satisfactory, the right can be reserved by the trustor in the trust instrument of exercising his discretion in altering, changing, or revoking the trust altogether.

Administrative Expense

It is provided in the federal estate tax law that expenses incurred in administering the estate of a deceased are deductible. Most of the states have a succession, inheritance, or a transfer tax which the recipients of the estate of the deceased will be expected to pay in accordance with the value of such property at the death of the deceased. The expense of administration will necessarily include fees of attorneys whose services are usually regarded by the executor or administrator as being essential. Fees paid attorneys for seeking a refund, in Cleveland v. Higgins,[1] were termed administrative expense and deductible.

Section 2053 of the *Federal Code* includes the following expenses which are deducted from the value of the gross estate before determining the taxable estate:

(a) Funeral expenses.
(b) Administrative expense.
(c) Claims against the estate.
(d) Unpaid mortgages.
(e) Marital rights.

In an Ohio[2] decision, fees paid an attorney for securing a construction of a will and for determining the federal estate tax were termed an administrative expense and deductible. Also, in a Pennsylvania[3] case, which was an early decision, the court ruled that the commissions paid executors and trustees, fees of attorneys in administering the estate, and the cost of a monument were deductible as a part of the funeral expenses of the deceased.

Exemptions from Tax

As a rule, the state court which has jurisdiction over the decedent's estate will determine the validity of the deduction for estate tax purposes. At a decedent's death in 1934, his son

[1] (DC NY), 50 F Supp 188 (1943).
[2] Schmalstig v. Conner, (DC Ohio), 46 F Supp 53 (1942).
[3] Loeb v. McCoughn, (DC Pa), 20 F 2d 1002 (1927).

presented to the executor a claim which was honored by the executor. It concerned an agreement to purchase 1,500 shares of stock from his father, the deceased, at its book value, and gave an interest-bearing note in payment. It was further stipulated that the note was to be paid from future accumulated dividends on the stock. The transfer was deductible under the statutory law of the state.[4]

The *1954 Internal Revenue Code*[5] defines deductions in the form of gifts: "In the case of gifts (other than gifts of future interests in property) made to any person by the donor during the calendar year 1955 and subsequent calendar years, the first $3,000 of such gifts shall not be included in the total amount of gifts made during such year." The *Code*[6] also describes losses arising from fires, storms, shipwrecks, other casualties, or from theft, when such losses are not compensated by insurance, as deductible from the gross estate for determining the amount of the taxable estate.

Consistent Policy of Giving

Various reasons might be offered in support of a donor's desire to make gifts to a minor for whom a feeling of responsibility is entertained. The immaturity of judgment of the minor, his meager income, and his deficiency in ownership of income-producing property may prompt a parent to help in remedying this situation and thus realize advantages from a tax point of view. Having decided to make some adjustment by way of improving the financial situation of another, the basic problem would be one of procedure in determining whether to make outright gifts to the minor or to establish a trust for providing him with the necessary income. In a trust arrangement, the exercise of controls over the minor would be feasible. By way of experimenting, the donor may create a revocable trust in which certain reservations are made involving the right to change, alter, or revoke the trust. Should the plan prove to be successful and satisfactory, the trustor may wish to substitute a nonrevocable trust for the revocable type.

In the case of a Colorado[7] father who had observed a consistent policy of making gifts to his children without any indication of approaching death in view of his seemingly enjoying good

---

[4] First Mechanics National Bank v. Com. of Int. Rev., (CCA 3), 117 F 2d 127 (1940).

[5] Section 2503.

[6] Ibid 2054.

[7] Colorado National Bank v. Com. of Int. Rev., 305 US 23, 83 L Ed 20 (1938).

health, the question of determining whether or not the transfers were made in contemplation of death was for the court to decide. The point was emphasized by the court that the mere fact a parent shows concern in making provision for the future welfare and comfort of his children does not establish conclusively that such an act was in contemplation of death.

In an effort to provide for the welfare of his children, a father, age 47, suffering from an incurable disease but, nevertheless, active in conducting his business, made gifts to his children. The court concluded, under the circumstances, that the gifts were absolute and not in contemplation of death. So long as the amount of the gifts came within the gift exemption, said the court, they were not to be considered as being taxable. Hence, the court ruled that the savings bonds purchased by the decedent for his daughters were not purchased in contemplation of death and were not taxable.[8]

Subject to Control of Trustor

In providing for the future welfare of one's wife or dependent children, the tendency repeatedly is instead of making the transfer to property absolute, to provide certain conditions, such as the attaining of a particular age, or upon the happening of a described contingency. When a trust is created and the trustor reserves the right to alter, change, or revoke the trust, such property remains a part of the gross estate of the trustor and will be subject to the estate tax upon his death. Even though this is a manner of providing for the future welfare of others, it will not necessarily represent a means of reducing the tax against the donor's estate at his death and, meanwhile, assure his heirs of their receiving eventually a greater amount of the estate.

A trustor transferred property in trust mainly as a safeguard against her own spendthrift tendencies while reserving all of the income to herself and, at the same time, granting to the trustees unlimited powers to invade the corpus for the well-being of the beneficiaries of the trustor. There was no certainty as to whether the remaindermen, consisting of her husband and children, would eventually receive any benefits. Under the circumstances, the court concluded that the statute pertaining to gifts did not apply.[9]

---

[8] Bsowarsky v. Granger (DC Pa), 148 F Supp 665 (1956).

[9] Com. of Int. Rev. v. Vander Weele, (CA 6), 254 F 2d 895 (1958).

Charitable Donations

A gift is not recognized by the law as being complete if it is in any way conditional and contingent. A statute upheld testamentary dispositions to charitable, religious, educational, and scientific organizations for estate tax deductions. The will of the deceased was probated in 1935. A deduction was made of $100,000 for a gift to an educational institution to be selected by the sister of the deceased and a $300,000 gift for a similar institution to be selected by his nephew. The evidence presented showed that these transfers had been discussed with the parties to whom the final decisions were conferred.

The will further provided that should the sister and nephew fail to indicate in writing within one year from the date of probation of the will describing such educational institutons as beneficiaries, it was directed that the legacies be considered as having lapsed and that the portions of the estate would be added to the residuary. No such designations as to transferees were made until October, 1935, at which time the name of the Labor Foundation, Inc. was submitted, and the $400,000 bequest was duly paid.

The court upheld the decision of the Commissioner in maintaining that a deductible gift requires that a testamentary transfer must be absolute and positive. There was an element of uncertainty connected with the promise of bequests. At the decedent's death, the unquestionable conveyances were dependent on the subsequent designations within one year thereof. Thus, the decision of the Commissioner not to allow the deductions was affirmed by the court.[10]

Testamentary gifts of the residue of the estate to charities, thereby giving the trustees the authority to apply the property to purposes other than to charities, was held in a St. Louis[11] decision not to be deductible. The court emphasized that the trustor had failed to confine the trustee to charities which were exclusively charitable. It was conceded that in some instances, the term "benevolent" is broader than the term "charity." One provision of the trust was on condition that a certain amount would be raised by the church before the trustees were allowed to depart with any portion of the corpus.

---

[10] Burdick et. al. v. Com. of Int. Rev., 117 F 2d 97 (1947).

[11] St. Louis Union Trust Co. v. Burnet, Com. of Int. Rev., (CCA 8) 59 F 2d 922 (1932).

Attorneys at law, in particular, are often concerned with ways and means of improving the standards of the legal profession. Thus, members of the profession who have acquired considerable wealth may desire to leave in their wills legacies to their particular bar associations. This type of legacy raises the question as to whether or not the amount so designated should be subject to the estate tax. Considering the objective of the bar association, a non-profit organization, intended for promoting high professional standards, courts have favored the theory that a transfer of this type aids in the promotion of a charitable motive, since it was in the interest of the public welfare, and should be considered deductible.

Conclusions drawn by courts favoring deductions for estate tax purposes in providing for legacies in the interest of promoting higher professional legal standards is in keeping with the *1954 Internal Revenue Code*[12] which states: "The value of the taxable estate shall be determined by deducting from the value of the gross estate the amount of all bequests, legacies, devises, or transfers (including the interest which falls into any such bequest, legacy, devise, transfer, or power) if the disclaimer is made before the date prescribed for the filing of the estate tax return."

Non-Taxable Gifts

Insofar as the gift tax statute is concerned, the time for making a gift or gifts is discretionary with the donor in that it can be given at one time or at any period during the donor's lifetime. The laws regulating gifts, testamentary transfers, and the creation of trusts are becoming more and more strict as a means of plugging up the loopholes in the tax structure and preventing individuals from disposing of their property beyond reason for the purpose of escaping the burden for the heirs of their estates.

Property transferred by a spouse to her husband pursuant to a property settlement in a Nevada[13] divorce decree was not taxable as a gift under the law of the state. While postnuptial property settlements are usually considered a subject of the federal gift tax, it was not so held in this instance. The court explained that the gift tax was intended to complement the federal estate tax in keeping the transferor from completely deplet-

[12] Section 2055 (a).

[13] Harris v. Com. of Int. Rev., 340 US 106, 95 L Ed 111 (1950).

ing his estate during his lifetime, thereby avoiding having to subject his estate to any tax whatsoever. However, both the estate tax and the gift tax do not include transfers for "an adequate and full consideration in money or money's worth."

Gifts to individuals during a particular year will not be declared subject to the gift tax unless the amount exceeds $3,000. The *Code* clarifies this provision: "In the case of gifts (other than gifts of future interest in property) made to any person by the donor during the calendar year 1955 and subsequent calendar years, the first $3,000 of such gifts to such person shall not be included in the total amount of gifts during such year."[14]

It is not difficult to visualize a situation of parents who are nearing the age of life expectancy and who have an urge to legally protect their estate, insofar as possible, for their children in providing a plan of making yearly gifts regularly to them. While observing a systematic system of making yearly gifts of the maximum deductible amount to each of four children, the amount of the estate transferred over a period of ten years will amount to $120,000 which will be tax-free of federal taxes. Should the wife join with her husband in the making of such gifts, the amount saved from taxes would be $240,000.

The $3,000 yearly gift tax exclusion for each of any number of donees has been retained in the 1976 TAX REFORM ACT, but the $30,000 lifetime gift exclusion ($60,000 if the other spouse joins in the giving) have been deleted.

Motives for Tax Savings

There perhaps would be little incentive for one to give away his property while he is living if there was not the possibility of his realizing any saving in death or gift taxes. On the other hand, there might be a strong tendency for him to exercise his personal control over his estate during his lifetime if it did not result in greater tax burdens at his death. This expectancy of saving in taxes will usually influence one in the careful planning of his estate.

Whenever the gift is executed, the donor is justified and entitled under the law in claiming certain exemptions. Gifts oftentimes are made at the expense of considerable sacrifice to the donor. It must not be overlooked that the donor takes great pride in asserting his right of ownership over his property

[14] Section 2503 (b), *1954 Internal Revenue Code.*

and in maintaining that it belongs to him. As a result, he experiences satisfaction in exercising the exclusive right to use his property as he desires.

A gift differs from a sale in that the lătter is a transfer of ownership to property. Of course, a tax is not imposed on a sale of property so long as the vendor receives full and adequate consideration in money or money's worth. When all requirements of a sale are fulfilled, there is no justification for the levying of any tax on the transaction.

Inter vivos gifts of one's wealth might be made for various reasons:

(a) Gifts to children in order to improve their financial security and independence.

(b) Transferring of property from the donor, who is in a comparatively high income tax bracket, to a donee, whose income is much smaller.

(c) For aiding and assisting children toward their securing the advantages of an education.

(d) Making possible the donee's entering a business or profession, resulting in his eventually becoming self-sufficient.

(e) Gifts in consideration of marriage, such as antenuptial or postnuptial contracts.

(f) Gifts in consideration of promises of a donee to refrain from further indulgence in certain bad habits until he reaches a definite age.

(g) Gifts to children in consideration of their promises to care for their parents the rest of their lifetime.

(h) Gifts to children as an inducement to their remaining at home for a reasonable period of time.

(i) While contemplating a second marriage, a parent may make gifts to his children so as not to deprive them of their shares of his estate.

(j) Making gifts in contemplation of death.

Associating Giving with Dying

After one has succeeded in acquiring the ownership of enough wealth to insure financial security in his old age, there will be little encouragement for him to dispose of his property through gifts to those for whom he entertains a moral obligation for their care and welfare. When he foresees the opportunity of possible protection of his estate from certain taxes at his death, he, no doubt, will become concerned with the various alternatives for enabling his beneficiaries to realize the greatest enjoyment in the future from his estate. In order that the anticipated saving in taxes can be accomplished, it becomes necessary to convince the Commissioner of Internal Revenue that the donor was not dominated with the fear of dying at the time of making the transfer.

The question which invariably arises whenever a gift of property is made concerns whether the gift was associated with living or was it made in anticipation of dying. The dominant motive for making a gift will determine if the gift is to be included in the gross estate of the deceased for tax purposes. A husband, who is beyond the retirement age and having entertained negative attitudes toward his health, made a donation of his straight life insurance policies to his wife who was financially independent. The court ruled that the gift was in contemplation of death and would have to be included in the decedent's gross estate for tax purposes.[15]

Marital Exemptions

Whether an individual's estate is considered small or unusually large, there naturally exists a strong urge on the owner's part to protect it, insofar as possible. Preceding the passage of the TAX REFORM ACT, the estate of every person, at the time of his death, was allowed an estate exemption of $60,000. A substitution for this procedure is a five-year phased-in credit allowance, beginning with the year 1977 of $30,000, which is the equivalent to a gross estate exemption of $120,000. According to the old tax statute, a married person with an estate of $120,000 would be able to claim an estate exemption of $60,000 plus $60,000 allowance for marital deduction, resulting in the estate of the deceased not being responsible for the payment of any estate tax. In the final results, the TAX REFORM ACT and the old tax statute are not very far apart.

Gifts are usually confined to one's spouse, his children, or other close relatives. The yearly gifts, not exceeding $3,000 for each of any number of individuals, or in the case of one's spouse of $6,000 each year, will be tax-free at the donor's

[15] Liebman v. Hassett, (DC Mass), (CCA 1), 148 F 2d 247, 50 F Supp 537 (1943).

death. Such gift allowances are made sufficiently large for covering gifts which ordinarily are made on special occasions, such as a legacy at the time of marriage, vacation time, Christmas, graduation, birthday, educational, or sight-seeing tour.

Marital deductions under the 1976 TAX REFORM ACT represent a few major changes. The wife is allowed tax-free exemptions for the first $100,000 in gifts, but the regular tax rate will apply to all gifts between $100,000 and $200,000. Amounts beyond $200,000 will be subject to the fifty per cent rate of marital deduction. After the death of one's spouse, the marital deduction rate has taken on a new dimension of either fifty per cent of the adjusted gross estate or $250,000, whichever is the larger.
cess allowances are taxed according to the gift tax rate which amounts to approximately 75 per cent of the estate tax. An important advantage in making large outright gifts of property is to save the difference in the gift tax and the subsequent estate tax rate. Also, the estate will be entitled to certain exemptions from the state inheritance or succession tax when the owner of property severs his relationship with it through the making of outright gifts.

Tax Allowances

Transfers of ownership of property as inter vivos gifts shall be listed in the return made by the donor for the particular calendar year. The so-called "taxable gifts" represent amounts in excess of the following deductions allowed:

(a) Gifts in excess of $3,000 to each donee, or $6,000 to each donee when one's spouse joins in the making of the gifts.

(b) $30,000 gift exemption during the lifetime of the donor, under the old law, or $60,000 if one's spouse signs a waiver, have been deleted in the 1976 TAX REFORM ACT.
$60,000 if the spouse signs his or her waiver.

(c) Gifts of the corpus of a trust for the benefit of the trustor's minor children represent future interests which are taxable; but the gifts of income each year as considered necessary by the trustee are regarded as present interests and are deductible.

The estate of the deceased beyond the $30,000 credit allowance (which is equivalent to an exemption of $120,000), as set forth in the 1976 TAX REFORM ACT, is subject to the federal estate tax. Such ownership will include property which is tangible and intangible, as well as that which is visible and invisible. In other words, all personal and real property, except real property located in some country other than the United States, will be included in the gross estate of the deceased for tax purposes.

The proceeds of life insurance policies payable to the estate of the deceased will be added to the taxable estate.

One will not be required to file a federal tax return during the five-year period when the $47,000 tax credit is being phased in unless the gross estate is beyond $120,000 in 1977; $134,000 in 1978; $147,000 in 1979; $161,000 in 1980; and $175,000 in 1981, as well as the following years. The estate of the deceased will be responsible for the payment of the estate tax; but by way of simplifying the procedure, the testator oftentimes provides for a residue out of which the estate tax is to be paid. While the state inheritance tax has to be paid by the beneficiaries, the testator may likewise arrange for the payment of the tax out of the residue and sometimes indicating certain beneficiaries who will be exempt from the inheritance tax.

Allowances for Previous Transfers

In the event of a beneficiary's death soon after the tranferor's death, resulting in double estate taxes having to be paid, the *1954 Internal Revenue Code*[16] allows full deduction for the taxes paid within two years from the time of the first decedent's death, and 20 per cent for every two subsequent years for the next ten years; but the allowance is not to be in excess of the value of the property received. The schedule of allowances is as follows:

(a) 80 percent if the transferor died within three or four years preceding the death of the decedent.
(b) 60 per cent if within the fifth or sixth years.
(c) 40 per cent if within the seventh or eighth years.
(d) 20 percent if within the ninth or tenth years.
(e) Should the decedent die more than ten years after the transferor's death, no credit will be allowed.

[16] Section 2013.

Chapter 21

Right of States to Tax

An inheritance or a succession tax represents a levy against the personal and real property which are received by the beneficiaries either by means of a last will and testament or under the law of descent and distribution after the death of the transferor. The amount of such tax to be shared by the beneficiaries will be in accordance with the proportion of the estate to which each beneficiary is entitled, in the absence of any provision to the contrary. Insofar as the tax rate is concerned, there is no system of uniformity existing in the various states. Yet, one can observe a close resemblance of tax procedures and tax rates in the different jurisdictions. The actual tax burden, of course, will be governed by the law of the transferor's state of domicile.

Privilege or Excise Tax

The distinction between an estate and an inheritance tax is that in the case of the former, the transferor exercises the privilege of determining to whom his property will go following his death, for which his estate is subject to tax; while in the latter, the transferee, as a rule, pays to the state an inheritance or a succession tax for the privilege of receiving and sharing in the estate of the deceased. Since the beneficiaries will gain from their receiving portions of the estate, they become responsible for the payment of the state inheritance tax. After all, who is better prepared than the beneficiaries to share in such an expenditure in view of their receiving property for which they have not made any contribution. It was recognized by the Supreme

Court[1] in an early decision that the power lies within the state to tax the property transferred by will, deed, or gift which is to take place following the death of the transferor. The court referred to the tax as a privilege or an excise tax rather than a property tax.

Some authorities are inclined to take a dim look at the various taxes which are imposed against the estate or the beneficiaries, since the payment of such taxes connotes a burden or a penalty. The tendency is to group all taxes on transfers of property according to the following categories: (1) gifts between living persons; (2) gifts in contemplation of impending death; (3) testamentary gifts; (4) transfers for full and adequate consideration in money or money's worth; and (5) providing for a life estate or possession until the happening of a certain contingency, after which the corpus will pass to the remainderman.

The executor or administrator is responsible for the payment of the state inheritance tax and other financial obligations of the estate to which the state is entitled. Prior to the beneficiary's receiving his portion of the estate, the executor will see to it that his share of the inheritance tax will be deducted at that time. Under no conditions could the beneficiary be required to participate in the payment of the tax should he refuse to acknowledge his right to the property.

Authority of States to Tax

In numerous instances, an estate is not sufficiently large to warrant the payment of a federal estate tax after the transferor's death because of the large exemption allowances. Thus, the estate becomes responsible only for the state inheritance tax. Whenever the estate of the deceased is rather large, it is quite a common practice for the testator to provide in his will the manner of paying the state inheritance tax out of the residue of the estate. Sometimes the amount received by the various beneficiaries will be quite nominal after the payment of burial expenses, attorney fees, executor or administrator's expenses, and court costs. Consequently, the ultimate benefits derived by beneficiaries can be quite disappointing. Occasionally, testators will provide in their wills for the payment of the abovementioned expenses out of the residue of the estate.

[1] Keeney v. Comptroller, 222 US 525, 56 L Ed 299, 32 S Ct 105 (1912).

The right of a state to tax the contingent remainder was taken to the Supreme Court[2] claiming that it was in violation of the "equal protection" clause and the "due process" clause contained in the Fourteenth Amendment. The New York statute provided for the payment of the tax by the life tenant at the testator's death and the subsequent payment of the tax by the contingent remainder after the death of the life tenant. The residue of the estate was originally bequeathed to the testator's widow for life. At her death, it was to be divided equally among the children and by per stirpes to the children of a deceased child. The imposing of a tax on the contingent remainder was interpreted by the court as not amounting to a violation of the "due process" clause or the "equal protection" clause of the Fourteenth Amendment.

Confusion as to Tax Jurisdiction

It has been contended that a tax levied by a state on an inheritance lacks uniformity, because the tax is based only on the property which is distributed during the particular year; but this theory was refuted by the Supreme Court[3] in an 1898 decision. The opinion expressed at that time was that an inheritance tax is not a tax on the property itself, but rather on its succession. The right to receive property by devise or descent instead of representing a natural right, was described as a creature of the law. Receiving property by devise or descent was concluded by the court as representing a privilege for which the state was justified in levying an inheritance tax.

Certain transfers of property within limitations as set forth in the statute are not subject to estate or inheritance taxes. There are specific exceptions which have to be observed, as described in the case of Heiner v. Donnan:[4] (1) the gifts must not have been made in contemplation of death; (2) a reservation must not have been made by the transferor; (3) the possession must have been transferred during the lifetime of the decedent; (4) it must have been given for full and adequate consideration in money or money's worth; and (5) the decedent must not have

---

[2] Saloman v. State Tax Com., 278 US 484, 73 L Ed 464, 49 S Ct 192 (1929).

[3] Magoun v. Illinois Savings Bank, 170 US 283, 42 L Ed 1037, 18 S Ct 594 (1898).

[4] Heiner v. Donnan, 285 US 312, 76 L Ed 772, 52 S Ct 358 (1932).

furnished the consideration with which to acquire the property.

The Supreme Court[5] recognized the right to the succession tax by the state representing the domicile of the deceased against the claim of another state in which some of the estate was located. Corrections can be made, under such circumstances, by filing an interpleader with the Supreme Court. At the time of the decedent's death, he was domiciled in Texas, but claims were also made by Florida, New York, and Massachusetts states, each of which claiming the right to tax the personal property located in the respective states regardless of the situs of the property. The court made clear that the purpose of the interpleader was to determine the state which is entitled to the state tax.

Source of Tax Fund

The state inheritance tax must be paid by the beneficiaries of the estate unless the testator prescribed the manner for making such payment. In the case of Leach v. Nichols,[6] the deceased died intestate, and the executor paid the estate tax in accordance with the Revenue Act of 1916. The Commissioner did not recognize a deduction from the gross estate for tax paid to the state of Massachusetts. The District Court allowed a recovery of the difference in the federal tax which was paid and what would have been paid if the deduction had been allowed for the payment of the state tax. The Circuit Court of Appeals denied this right to recover. The Supreme Court affirmed the decision of the Circuit Court of Appeals in maintaining that the state inheritance tax is paid by the parties who receive the property of the deceased. Thus, the state tax, which was paid by the executor for the sake of convenience, must subsequently be paid by the beneficiaries.

The inheritance tax is described in the decision of Goadman v. Granger,[7] as a levy on the privilege of receiving property of the estate of the deceased. In contrast with the federal estate tax which is based on the actual value of the taxable estate of the deceased, the inheritance tax is calculated on the distributive share of the decedent's estate.

---

[5] Worcester County Trust Co. v. Riley, 302 US 292, 82 L Ed 268, 58 S Ct 185 (1937).

[6] 285 US 165, 76 L Ed 681 (1932).

[7] 335 US 835, 2 L Ed 2d 47, 78 S Ct 57 (1957).

While the general rule is that the inheritance tax is paid by the beneficiaries, the testator has the authority to prescribe the residuary of the estate out of which the inheritance tax will be paid. In the absence of any directive to the contrary, the responsibility for the payment of the inheritance tax, according to the precedent established in most states, falls on the beneficiaries in proportion to the amount of the estate received. As a result, the portion of the tax burden of each beneficiary will be deducted from his share of the estate.

The state that has jurisdiction over the person has been recognized as having the authority to tax the personal property of a deceased regardless of its location. A contrary view is taken as to the right to tax real property located in another state. The Supreme Court[8] refused to recognize the right to go beyond the state in collecting inheritance tax on lands and chattels. The state is which the real property is located has the right to determine the inheritance tax and not the state claiming the domicile of the deceased.

Tax on Personal Property

It has been decided by the Supreme Court that money of the deceased, even though the amount is small or is located in another state, is subject to the inheritance tax in the state of the domicile of the owner and not the state of the situs. A bank deposit has been recognized by the courts as representing a chose in action against which an inheritance tax is assessed by the state in which the deceased claimed as his place of domicile rather than the state where the bank is located.

The facts revealed that the state of domicile of the deceased was Connecticut; and at the time of his death, he owned a considerable tangible estate outside the state of his domicile, including an interest as a general partner in a New York firm, besides other financial ownership in the state of New York. The Supreme Court[9] took the position that a succession tax is not a tax on the property, but rather a tax on the privilege to the succession of such property. The state of the domicile of the deceased was declared to have the right to impose the succession

---

[8] City Bank Farmers Trust Co. v. Schander, 291 US 24, 78 L Ed 628, 54 S Ct 259 (1934).

[9] Blodgett v. Silberman, 277 US 1, 72 L Ed 749, 48 S Ct 410 (1927).

tax on intangible property even though it was located outside the state.

In determining the state which has the right to tax personal property of the deceased, the court held in a Minnesota[10] case that personal property held by the deceased was subject to the inheritance tax in the state in which the deceased claimed as his domicile. The deceased, a resident of New York, died intestate in 1925. He held bonds and certificates of indebtedness issued by the state of Minnesota and the cities of Minneapolis and St. Paul valued at $300,000. When the will was probated in New York, a state tax was levied against the testamentary transfer of property including out-of-state securities. Minnesota also assessed a tax on the inheritance issued in that state. The Supreme Court held that the Minnesota bonds and securities had a permanent location in New York state, which made them taxable in that state due to the state's having jurisdiction of the owner.

From the standpoint of a state's constitutional authority to levy an inheritance tax, it is recognized that a state may go to the extreme in making such a tax excessive. In the state of California,[11] the estate of the deceased amounted to $1,800,000 against which a federal estate tax of more than $128,000 was levied. In determining the amount of the estate against which the state of California could levy an inheritance tax, the tax appraiser did not allow a deduction for the federal estate tax. As a result, the state inheritance tax assessed against the residuary amounted to more than $26,000 due to no allowance or deduction for the estate tax from the gross estate before calculating the inheritance tax. The state courts maintained that the "due process" or "equal protection" clauses of the Fourteenth Amendment had not been violated, and this viewpoint was affirmed by the Supreme Court.

Rights Reserved by Testator

When one makes a gift of property while living, he frequently will exercise his right of reserving the power of altering, changing, or revoking the transfer. In concluding whether the property formerly disposed of will be subject to the death tax at the

[10] Farmers Loan Co. v. Minnesota, 280 US 204, 74 L Ed 371, 50 S Ct 98 (1930).

[11] Stebbins v. Riley, 268 US 137, 69 L Ed 884, 45 S Ct 424 (1925).

decedent's death, the various conditions will be considered, such as: age, marriage or remarriage, right to change one's mind, deaths, births, or upon the happening of some specified contingency. Whenever a transfer is made with a reversionary right attached, the property must be included in the gross estate of the transferor at his death because of the possibility that the possession might have reverted back to the transferor or his estate.

A state is recognized by the courts as having the power to tax not only the property included in the estate of the deceased at the time of death, but also the right to tax economic interests in property of others as a result of death. A decedent who resided in New Jersey moved to New York and created a trust naming a New York corporation as trustee. The trust was irrevocable, and no control over the property was reserved by the trustor. It provided for the payment of income over to the trustor during his lifetime and then to his wife for her life, should she survive him, with the corpus subsequently to be divided equally among his two sons. The trustor was predeceased by his wife, and death came to the trustor in 1936.

The New Jersey Commissioner contended that the trust constituted equitable contingent remainders in the sons; and while the trustor was domiciled in New Jersey, the transfers were made in contemplation of death and, therefore, taxable. This decision was affirmed by the Supreme Court.[12]

A controversy which faced the Oklahoma[13] courts was whether property which was held in trust by the United States Government should be subject to the inheritance tax of Oklahoma. The facts concerned a full-blooded Oklahoma Indian who died intestate in 1941. His mother survived him and was his sole heir. The net estate of the deceased was estimated to be in excess of $111,000, against which a tax and penalty amounted to more than $5,000. It was held that the state of Oklahoma had the authority to levy an inheritance tax on property held in trust by the United States Government for the benefit of the deceased.

[12] Central Hanover Bank & Trust Co. v. Kelly, 319 US 94, 87 L Ed 1282, 63 S Ct 945 (1943).

[13] West v. Oklahoma Tax Com., 334 US 717, 92 L Ed 1676, 68 S Ct 1223 (1948).

Chapter 22

Tax Computations and Procedures

A vital subject of increasing importance to all individuals is that of taxes. Because of a strong tendency on the part of the taxpayers to escape, through the use of legal technicalities, from having to make such payments, lawmakers have been constantly endeavoring to amend the tax structure, thereby making it increasingly difficult for one to by-pass his duty to pay. Nevertheless, there is nothing irregular or illegal in one's analyzing his own tax problems in an effort to alleviate his tax burden, insofar as possible. In order to cope more successfully with the tax situation, particularly for one who possesses a large ownership, it is highly important for such a person to familiarize himself with the various alternatives for meeting his tax obligations in order to be better equipped for acting intelligently and wisely in planning his estate.

Current Tax Situations

Taxes, of course, have to be levied for the purpose of raising revenue for the support and maintenance of the functions of our federal and state governments. Most individuals, as a rule, who are concerned with the subject of death taxes are inclined to favor any taxing procedures for acquiring funds to be used for public service when they are not adversely affected, while registering considerable displeasure when any tax proposal is introduced which will have a tendency to somewhat deplete the financial content of their pocketbooks.

Whenever property is involved, taxes, one type or another, are constantly being imposed under varied circumstances:

(a) When one acquires the ownership of property by inheritance, deductions will be made for the privilege of acquiring it.
(b) In maintaining one's right of ownership over personalty or realty, a personal property tax or a real estate tax will have to be paid annually.
(c) A sales tax is imposed against the vendee when property is acquired in a sales transaction.
(d) Taxes are levied on the income from wages, salary, or investments.
(e) A gift tax is imposed against an outright gift of property whenever the value is in excess of the allowed deductions.
(f) A federal estate tax is charged against the estate of a deceased in return for the testator's privilege of determining to whom such property will descend after his death.

Federal Taxes on Estates

The federal gift tax approaches approximately 75 per cent of the federal estate tax. A disadvantage, or course, to the donor's making an inter vivos gift is his being deprived of the pleasure of using the property and in exercising his ownership and control over it during the rest of his lifetime. Furthermore, after having made the transfer, certain unforeseen personal and financial situations might occur that would present a cause for the donor's regretting the rather premature decision to make a transfer for the sake of gaining some tax advantages, as well as reducing the over-all future income taxes due to the differences in the income brackets of the donor and the donee.

One noteworthy distinction in the federal taxes (estate and gift) and the state inheritance tax is that in the former, the estate is responsible for the tax payments, while in the latter, the legatees and devisees are liable for the tax unless the testator indicated the source from which the death taxes would be paid; namely, a general or a residuary fund.

Alternatives of Transferor

The owner of property has several possibilities for making transfers of his estate either while he is living or to become effective at his death:

(a) He may choose to follow the line of least resistance in failing to make a will, thereby relying on the law of descent and distribution for the prorating of his estate following his death. This procedure is not only unsatisfactory taxwise, but also the distribution of the property will have to be made in such a manner which in all probability would not meet the approval of the deceased had he been living. Meanwhile, the needs of those for whom the deceased was primarily responsible would not be met adequately. The widow (according to statutory provisions) ordinarily would be entitled to only one-third of the estate, while the children would receive the other two-thirds.

(b) One can make a testamentary transfer of his entire estate to designated beneficiaries. Since the ownership of property is constantly changing, it is important that the testator update his will from time to time or a codicil be prepared for indicating additions to or deletions from his estate.

(c) The entire estate can be left unconditionally to one's surviving spouse; and, except where the estate is more than $500,000, no estate tax would have to be paid. In comparatively smaller estates, no federal estate tax would have to be paid if the amount left to the surviving spouse did not amount to more than the $250,000 marital deduction.

(d) In order to take full advantage of the marital deduction of one-half of the taxable gross estate or $250,000, whichever is the larger, in accordance with the 1976 TAX REFORM ACT, the surviving spouse would not be responsible for paying any federal estate tax at the death of the deceased provided the taxable estate, after all deductions were made, did not exceed $250,000.

(e) Particularly when the estate is quite large, the transferor may wish to observe a policy of liquidating a part of his estate while he is living and escape both federal and estate taxes. The federal gift tax statute permits the making of unconditional gifts of $3,000 each year to each of any number of donees.

Should the wife join her husband in making gifts, thus releasing some of her rights to his estate, the yearly gift becomes doubled. In other words, the $3,000 tax-free gifts to each of any number of persons will be increased to $6,000. Furthermore, yearly gifts to one's spouse are tax free to the extent of $6,000.

(f) Should a spouse wish not to leave property outright to his dependents, this can be accomplished by way of creating a testamentary trust, thereby transferring the title to the designated property at the testator's death to a trustee who will be responsible for executing the wishes of the transferor according to the provisions set forth in his will.

Tax on Trusts

Prior to the passage of the *1954 Internal Revenue Code*, individuals possessing large estates, in particular, were concerned with ways and means of protecting their property, following their deaths, from being subjected to the federal estate tax and also the state inheritance tax by making inter vivos transfers of ownership. This loophole was corrected by the following statutory provision: "The gift tax shall apply, whether the transfer is in trust or otherwise, whether the gift is direct or indirect, and whether the property is real or personal, tangible, or intangible; but in the case of a non-resident not a citizen of the United States, it shall apply to a transfer only if the property is situated within the United States."[1]

In the state of Florida,[2] a man with considerable wealth created an irrevocable trust in favor of his wife in consideration of her agreement to release all dower claims to her husband's estate as his wife. The court reasoned that the consideration was inadequate in money or money's worth to grant an exemption from the gift tax statute. The husband had been married twice. His estate consisted of $5,000,000 in cash and securities and $135,000 in real estate.

The antenuptial agreement provided for the husband's setting up an irrevocable trust of $300,000 in conformity with her wishes. Two other trusts of similar amounts were to be made testamentary, one of which was to be similar to the inter vivos trust and the other was to provide for the care of his children. In return, the wife was to release her husband from her marital

[1] Section 2511 (a), *1954 Internal Revenue Code*.

[2] Merrill v. Fahs, Col. of Int. Rev., 324 US 308, 89 L Ed 963 (1945).

rights. The Commissioner claimed that a gift tax was due on the transfer of $300,000 in trust. The District Court sustained the taxpayer's action for a gift tax refund; but the decision was reversed by the Circuit Court of Appeals. In the decision of the Supreme Court, which affirmed the decision of the Circuit Court of Appeals, Mr. Justice Frankfurter stated that failure to apply the gift tax statute to such a transfer would encourage a tax avoidance.

Factors Influencing Gifts

Unless one's estate is quite large, there is little incentive for the average person to resort to an inter vivos transfer of his property which would result in all control, as well as all rights of ownership, being surrendered. The possibility of realizing tax exemptions through gifts while living in order to reduce the estate tax at the time of one's death deserves careful consideration. Besides, the gift tax rate is equivalent to approximately three-fourths of the estate tax rate.

The federal gift tax must be paid each year on the net gifts. A deduction is allowed the donor of $3,000 in money or money's worth for each of any number of donees during any particular year.

The so-called $30,000 lifetime gift exemption has been deleted by the 1976 TAX REFORM ACT.

Transfers for Adequate Consideration

The value of the property at the time of the gift, according to the *1954 Internal Revenue Code*,[3] will be the basis for determining the amount of gift tax which must be paid: "When property is transferred for less than an adequate and full consideration in money or money's worth, the amount by which the value of the property exceeded the value of the consideration shall be deemed a gift and shall be included in computing the amount of gifts made during the calendar year."

One might be inclined to presume that whenever the owner of property is directed by the court to transfer the ownership to a dependent, such a transfer will be for full and adequate consideration in money or money's worth and not subject to the gift tax. In the case of Commissioner of Internal Revenue v. Greene,[4] the court, in ordering the transfer of property belonging to an incompetent person to his own child, interpreted

---

[3] Section 2512 (b).

[4] 314 US 641, 86 L Ed 514, 62 S Ct 80 (1941).

the transaction as a taxable gift.

In determining the gift tax on a life insurance policy, which had been paid-up through the installment plan, the value of the transfer, in the case of Houston v. Commissioner of Internal Revenue,[5] was the replacement cost had the taxpayer at the time of the gift secured a single premium paid-up policy for the particular amount. The replacement cost was determined by the amount which would be charged for a single premium life insurance policy for the amount involved when considering the present age of the applicant.

In 1934, the taxpayer made a gift of five fully-paid life insurance policies. It was the contention of the taxpayer that the gift tax should be based on the cash surrender value at the time of the transfer. The Commissioner took the position that the replacement value must be the basis for determining the gift tax. The court concluded that the cost of replacement was the more logical criterion for judging the value of the policies.

Applying Gift Tax Statute

The statute provides that each year, subsequent to 1955, a gift tax will be imposed on the transfer of property as a gift by a person, whether resident or non-resident, except for the transfer of intangible property by one not a citizen of the United States nor engaged in business in the United States during the particular calendar year. Except for the limited exceptions, the gift tax applies to all such transfers even those which are made to a trustee in a trust relationship for designated beneficiaries.

The donor is responsible for the payment each year of the gift tax on the net gifts for the particular year exceeding $3,000 in money or money's worth to any number of individuals.

The estate tax exemption of $60,000, and the gift tax exemption of $30,000 distributed over the donor's lifetime, have been unified into a single rate schedule covering both the estate transferred at the death of the owner and gifts made during the owner's lifetime.

In the event the donor dies prior to the filing of a return and the payment of the tax, the executor or administrator will have the responsibility of collecting the tax fund from the donees according to the proportionate amount of the gift transfers.

---

[5] (CCA 3), 124 F 2d 518 (1941).

COMPARATIVE ESTATE & GIFT TAX RATES

Taxable Estates and Gifts	Not More Than	Estate Tax Rates Before 1977	Gift Tax Rates Before 1977	1977 Single Unified Tax Rates
$ -----	$ 5,000	3%	2¼%	18%
5,000	10,000	7	5¼	18
10,000	20,000	11	8¼	20
20,000	30,000	14	10½	22
30,000	40,000	18	13½	22
40,000	50,000	22	16½	24
50,000	60,000	25	18¾	24
60,000	80,000	28	21	26
80,000	100,000	28	21	28
100,000	150,000	30	22½	30
150,000	250,000	30	22½	32
250,000	500,000	32	24	34
500,000	750,000	35	26¼	37
750,000	1,000,000	37	27¾	39
1,000,000	1,250,000	39	29¼	41
1,250,000	1,500,000	42	31½	43
1,500,000	2,000,000	45	33¼	45
2,000,000	2,500,000	49	36¾	49
2,500,000	3,000,000	53	39¾	53
3,000,000	3,500,000	56	42	57
3,500,000	4,000,000	59	44¼	61
4,000,000	4,500,000	63	47¼	65
4,500,000	5,000,000	63	47¼	69
5,000,000	6,000,000	67	50¼	70
6,000,000	7,000,000	70	52½	70
7,000,000	8,000,000	73	54¾	70
8,000,000	10,000,000	76	57	70
10,000,000	----------	77	57¾	70

FEDERAL ESTATE TAX

Estate Tax Deductions

As a convenience in having available funds necessary for paying estate taxes, the insured when applying for a life insurance policy might arrange for his estate, or his executor, to be named the beneficiary in order to provide for adequate funds with which to pay the death taxes on his estate. While this practice would offer advantages for meeting tax obligations, it, nevertheless, might prove to be quite expensive, since the proceeds will be included in the gross estate for tax purposes.

In keeping with the 1976 TAX REFORM ACT for phasing in, over a five-year period, the necessary credit for 1977 and subsequent years, the procedure to be observed will be as follows:

Year	*Credit Allowance*	*Equivalent Exemptions*
1977	30,000	120,000
1978	34,000	134,000
1979	39,000	147,000
1980	42,500	161,000
1981	47,000	175,000

The TAX REFORM ACT of 1976 combines the federal estate and gift tax rates into a single unified rate schedule, thus necessitating the elimination of the lifetime gift exemption of $30,000, which represented a deduction before determining the amount of the gift tax as well as the $60,000 exemption as applied to the federal estate tax. As a result of the single unified estate and gift tax credits taking the place of the old estate and gift tax exemptions, there will be a fewer number of estates hereafter that will be required to file the single unified estate and gift tax return. The new law also offers greater leniency to those who might otherwise experience considerable difficulty in paying estate and gift taxes, by way of allowing additional time in which to pay. In the event a farm or a business is involved, the time for meeting the tax obligation may be distributed over a fifteen-year period at a low interest rate of four per cent for the first one million dollars.

SINGLE UNIFIED ESTATE & GIFT TAX SCHEDULE

Taxable Estates and Gifts	*Not More Than*	*Tax Rate*	*Tax*	*In Excess*
$ ------	$ 10,000	18%	$ ------	$ ------
10,000	20,000	20	1,800	10,000
20,000	40,000	22	3,800	20,000
40,000	60,000	24	8,200	40,000
60,000	80,000	26	13,000	60,000
80,000	100,000	28	18,200	80,000
100,000	150,000	30	23,800	100,000
150,000	250,000	32	38,800	150,000
250,000	500,000	34	70,800	250,000
500,000	750,000	37	155,800	500,000
750,000	1,000,000	39	248,300	750,000
1,000,000	1,250,000	41	345,800	1,000,000
1,250,000	1,500,000	43	448,300	1,250,000
1,500,000	2,000,000	45	555,800	1,500,000
2,000,000	2,500,000	49	780,800	2,000,000
2,500,000	3,000,000	53	1,025,800	2,500,000
3,000,000	3,500,000	57	1,290,800	3,000,000
3,500,000	4,000,000	61	1,575,800	3,500,000
4,000,000	4,500,000	65	1,880,800	4,000,000
4,500,000	5,000,000	69	2,205,800	5,000,000
5,000,000	---------	70	2,550,800	5,000,000

CREDITING STATE INHERITANCE TAX

Allowances for Inheritance Tax

The federal government offers encouragement to the various states to enact death tax statutes for raising revenue. Certain deductions are made possible in meeting the federal estate obligation based on the amount of the federal estate tax. Such a tax allowance presents a challenge to the states to consider the adoption of statutes for taxing the estates of deceased persons in order to take full advantage of the federal allowances.

FEDERAL ALLOWANCES FOR STATE INHERITANCE TAXES

Taxable Estate	*Not More Than*	*Tax*	*Tax Rate*	*In Excess*
------	40,000	---		
40,000	90,000	---	.8%	40,000
90,000	140,000	400	1.6	90,000
140,000	240,000	1,200	2.4	140,000
240,000	440,000	3,600	3.2	240,000
440,000	640,000	10,000	4.0	440,000
640,000	840,000	18,000	4.8	640,000
840,000	1,040,000	27,600	5.6	840,000
1,040,000	1,540,000	38,800	6.4	1,040,000
1,540,000	2,040,000	70,800	7.2	1,540,000
2,040,000	2,540,000	106,800	8.0	2,040,000
2,540,000	3,040,000	146,800	8.8	2,540,000
3,040,000	3,540,000	190,800	9.6	3,040,000
3,540,000	4,040,000	238,800	10.4	3,540,000
4,040,000	5,040,000	290,800	11.2	4,040,000
5,040,000	6,040,000	402,800	12.0	5,040,000
6,040,000	7,040,000	522,800	12.8	6,040,000
7,040,000	8,040,000	650,800	13.6	7,040,000
8,040,000	9,040,000	786,800	14.4	8,040,000
9,040,000	10,040,000	930,800	15.2	9,040,000
10,040,000	---------	1,082,800	16.0	10,040,000

In view of the tax concessions made by the federal government on state inheritance taxes, a greater amount of cooperation and harmony between the federal government and the various states is encouraging. To qualify for this federal assistance, a state, first of all, must have a statute taxing the estates of deceased persons. Since the obligation of an estate to the federal government is lowered because of the allowances, without the imposing of any additional burden on the states, it becomes easier for the beneficiaries of the estate to meet their inheritance tax obligations to the states.

In determining the amount of taxes due the federal and state governments, the general plan of procedure is to first discover the federal estate tax, after which the state inheritance tax becomes simpler to calculate. While the estate tax on a farm or a closely-held business is expected to be paid within a period of nine months following the owner's death, arrangements can be made to somewhat lessen the tax burden by distributing the payments over a period of fifteen years. This procedure amends the old regulations which permitted the executor to distribute the payments of the estate tax on such property over a period of ten years. Arrangements can also be made for not paying any of the estate tax for the first five years, and to pay only the interest. When this plan is observed, the estate tax payments must be distributed over the remaining ten years.

Filing Tax Returns

A gift (other than a future interest) made to a donee of more than $3,000 during any calendar year must be filed on a gift tax return form number 709 on or before April 15 of the following year. The filing of the return, along with the payment of the tax, shall be made at the nearest office of the District Director of Internal Revenue in the area in which the donor claims as his place of domicile.

The estate tax return must be filed on form number 706 before the expiration of the fifteen month period after the decedent's death. Payment of the tax shall be made at the office of the District Director of Internal Revenue in the particular area. Under the old regulations pertaining to the filing of a gift tax return for amounts in excess of a $3,000 gift to each of any number of individuals, or in making any future gift, a gift tax return had to be filed in each calendar year in which there had been a gift regardless of the amount.

The present regulations for gifts under the 1976 TAX REFORM ACT require a quarterly gift tax return only when taxable gifts are made during the quarter, along with other gifts during the year which have not been reported, amount to more than $25,000. Whenever the taxable gifts during the year are not greater than $25,000, a gift tax return must be filed by February 15 of the following year. Within two months after the death of the deceased, or after the confirmation of the executor's nomination, or the appointment of the administrator, should the gross estate for tax purposes exceed the allowed deduction, notice of the death must be given to the Office of the Collector of Internal Revenue on tax form 704.

INDEX